Delight in Disorder:
Ministry, Madness, Mission

by

Tony Roberts

A Way With Words Publishing is a mission designed to help people discover divine delight in a disordered world.

For mission updates, go to our website – www.awaywithwordsforyou.com

ISBN: 978-0-9718038-8-6

Cover design by Nicole Miller
Edited by Leanne Sype
Poems by Matthew Pullar

Roberts, Tony.
    Delight in Disorder/ Tony Roberts.
    Includes bibliographical references.
ISBN: 978-0-9718038-8-6
        1.   Mental   illness—Religious   aspects—
    Christianity. 2. Mentally ill—Religious life. I. Title.

"Dear children, let us not love with words or speech
but with actions and in truth…"
(1 John 3:18)

~ For Alice ~

Here are the words and the truth. I'm still working
on the actions. Bear with me.

Acknowledgments

One lesson I learned in seminary is not to inflict the sum total of your theology in your first sermon. Otherwise, you might not get the opportunity for a second.

In this spirit, I want to thank God for just some of the people who led me to *Delight in Disorder* and encouraged me to keep at it until I could share with you.

~ My children - Sarah, Grace, Caleb, and Hannah. Sadly, you've been more the subjects of my stories than the objects of my affection. I love you more than I've allowed myself to express.

~ The people, the churches (especially Zion Presbyterian, Cochranton Presbyterian, Ovid Federated, and Greenlawn Presbyterian), the governing bodies, and the Board of Pensions of the Presbyterian church (U.S.A.) who provided for me and my family financially and in so many other ways.

~ Marlin Freed, a family minister, who discipled me through dark days when the project was conceived.

~ My dad and his wife Connie, my mom and her husband Dan, as well as my sister April and her husband Dan who lavished me with praise and bought me my trusty laptop.

~ Readers of my now-defunct blog *Necessary Therapy* who read early drafts and provided helpful comments. Also, readers of my now emerging blog *A Way With Words* who keep me writing nearly every day.

~ Dr. Jennifer Gunn who helped me maintain chemical balance and Jeff Nottingham who guided me back to my moral compass.

~ The people of Grace church PCA in Rochester, New York and the Columbus Reformed Presbyterian church for providing me spiritual homes away from home.

~ My uncle Larry and my aunt Linda, who shared their beautiful retreat condo where, after four years of a difficult pregnancy, I enjoyed fruitful labor. My aunt Rosialene and uncle Richard for finding a laptop case to suit my taste – high quality at a garage sale price.

~ Elizabeth Mellencamp-Johnson for freely offering the inspired subtitle.

~ Nicole Miller of Miller Media Solutions for the delightfully disordered cover.

~ My personal editor Leanne Sype of *Pen to Paper Communications*. Leanne helped shape the disorder of my dilapidated mind into a house that makes beautiful sense.

Table of Contents

The Living Room

Victory over Our Enemies
Desert Wastes
To a Spacious Place
Where is He?
Good Boundaries
Good Friday
The Great Therapist
Living Promise
Intimate with God
Night Time Terror, Day Time Destruction
A Breath
Shining Face
Rest for Your Weary Soul
The Wrath of the LORD
Divine Restraint
A Level Path
What We Need, When We Need It
A Manic Creation
Coming Home
A Day for Rejoicing
The Great Congregation
Living to Tell About It

The Basement

Crying
Being Humbled
Confined by God
Out of the Pit
The Past is Past
Long Dead
From the Depths of the Earth
Remembering
From the Depths of Sheol
Afflicted

Delight in Misery
An E.C.T. Morning
In the Shelter of the Most High

The Prayer Closet

No Comfort
Speechless
In the Shadow
Meditate and Moan
I Hate to Complain, But…
Help!
Defenseless
Silent Pondering
Cheer Up
Divine Remembering
Divine Satisfaction

The Kitchen

Highways: Lost and Found
Tumult
Abundance
Prisoners in Misery
Happy or Blessed?
Ten Reasons to Leave Your Psychiatrist
Ten Things to Look for in a Psychiatrist
How Long?
Consolation Surprise
Revive Us Again
Preparing the Table

The Study

From One Unquiet Mind to Another
The Dream Team is a Nightmare
Song for Vincent Reconsidered

Foreword

Tony Roberts' book is not the first I've read by an ordained clergyman diagnosed with bipolar disorder. Some years back, a renowned (former) mega-church pastor/motivational speaker began his tome by declaring, "I have conquered bipolar disorder." Right... What makes Tony's devotional so compelling is that bipolar disorder continues to periodically beat the crap out of him, and he still believes. He still sees God working in his life, finds himself slowly but surely transforming despite, and even through, the torment of this disease. This level of honesty and vulnerability is rare, and if you're seeking hope and understanding in the midst of the painful and messy parts of life, do like me and hop on the Tony Roberts train.

Tony Roberts has a way with words. With the gifts of a poet and the precision of a surgeon, he skillfully zeroes in on the dilemmas so many of us believers who contend with brain disease (25 percent of us) face each and every day. I've been scribbling quotes throughout my reading, and if I were a lesser mortal, I'd scoop them up and claim them as my own. I don't want to quote him here because if you're anything like me, you'll want to uncover these gems, one at a time, as you read, reflect and then read some more. The wise Seattle writer Naomi Stenberg once remarked, "One can be much more accepting of one's (mental illness) when one is not tormented by it." Tony Roberts takes it a step further and proposes that one can find delight in the disorder. God, Tony demonstrates – again and again – can work in the midst of the worst chaos, the most overwhelming pain.

As a mental health advocate with over 25 years of experience, I've long understood the circle of empathy in faith communities rarely extends to individuals and families carrying the burden of serious and persistent mental illness. Ironically, our churches are filled with hurting people; so many of them hiding these very same wounds. When clergymen speak, people often listen. I hope you find yourself as challenged and rewarded by reading Tony Roberts' splendid devotional book. If you have the means, buy a copy for your church pastor too.

David Zucker
Mental Health Advocate
University Presbyterian Church
Seattle, WA.
11/28/13

Introduction: No Escaping God

Where can I go from your Spirit?
Where can I flee from your presence?
If I go up to the heavens, you are there;
If I make my bed in the depths, you are there. (Psalm 139:7-8)

I had the good fortune and the awful burden of growing up in a family that taught me the fear of the LORD. Though this fear was not always healthy (or always faithful to Scripture), it did anchor me through rough waters and kept me growing in a love-relationship with God through Jesus Christ. Since before my birth, God has been busy pursuing me. I have strayed, yet I've always been kept within the range of God's never-failing love.

We all experience ups and downs in life. But with bipolar disorder, my highs have been dangerously high and my lows critically low. At both extremes, I have flirted with death, coming very close to ending my life and doing great damage to those around me. Through miraculous mercy, God has kept me alive, saving me from certain destruction.

For over 30 years of my often reckless life, the Psalms have helped me maintain spiritual balance.

As a chaplain, I recited Psalms in community each morning during prayer service. In my quiet time, I've regularly read and reflected on the Psalms in writing. In weekly worship, Psalms shine through the hymns and praise songs I've selected and sung. On retreats, I've joined brothers and sisters in Christ as they've read the Psalms in prayer and over meals.

The title of this book is partially taken from a poem by Robert Herrick. It is not about God or bipolar disorder.

1

Instead, it is about a dress. But more than a dress.

A sweet disorder in the dress
Kindles in clothes a wantonness:
A lawn about the shoulders thrown
Into a fine distraction:
An erring lace which here and there
Enthrals the crimson stomacher:
A cuff neglectful, and thereby
Ribbons to flow confusedly:
A winning wave (deserving note)
In the tempestuous petticoat:
A careless shoe-string, in whose tie
I see a wild civility:
Do more bewitch me than when art
Is too precise in every part. [1]

There is a "wild civility" to bipolar disorder that makes it deceptively desirable at times.

Before I was diagnosed with bipolar, I was mired in the darkness of despair, unable to accomplish anything, sleeping through the day and lying awake in bed at night. I was prescribed an anti-depressant which brought almost instantaneous relief.

Suddenly, I was able to wake up early, spend a tremendous deal of concentrated time in prayer and Scripture and write. Oh, could I write! I was divinely inspired (or so I thought). I wrote a book on prayer in little over a week, staying up late nights and waking up early in the mornings, leaving behind my wife and infant daughter so I could pursue the muse. It felt great. But it was awful. I was delightfully disordered.

The "sweet disorder" of the dress Herrick describes is

preferred over more "precise art." There is something incredibly alluring about the intensity experienced, particularly during manic phases of bipolar. Mania (or its more gentle sister "hypomania") can induce fits of creativity that seem (and may well be) tremendously productive. But there is a cost. There is truth in the tired cliché, "What goes up, must come down." More than this, when I have allowed myself to go up, I have often left important people behind.

Yet, there is genuine "delight" to be found in bipolar disorder, and this is the story I most want to tell in this book. Delight is first an expression of God's love for us.

[God] brought me out into a spacious place;
he rescued me because he delighted in me. (Psalm 18:19)

Countless times, when I have been driven to the edge of a cliff, God has rescued me and set me on level ground. Why would God do this? Because God delights in me, even in my disorder.

Since God delights in us, we have a "delightful duty" to share in God's joy.

May those who delight in my vindication
shout for joy and gladness;
may they always say, "The LORD be exalted,
who delights in the well-being of his servant." (Psalm 35:27)

Of course, there are some disorderly occasions when delight seems humanly impossible, and even irresponsibly cruel. I write this just one week after 27-year old Matthew Warren, son of Rick Warren (author of the best-selling *The Purpose-Driven Life*) committed suicide. Now is not the time to delight, at least from a human perspective. The Bible tells us to "mourn with those who mourn." We grieve our loss in Matthew's death, with the Warren family and all of his loved ones left behind.

Still, it is important, even essential to somehow come back to delight. As the Apostle Paul writes,

... give thanks in all circumstances; for this is God's will for you in Christ Jesus. (1 Thessalonians 5:18)

We give thanks *in* all circumstances, not *for* all circumstances. Matthew's death was a terrible tragedy. The suffering endured by countless people who battle mental illness daily (and sometimes lose the fight) is not something for which we should be grateful.

Yet, for their sake, for our own sake, for Christ's sake, we can (and should) delight in the disorder—call on the presence of God when God seems absent, point to the light of Christ in the darkness, share in the Spirit of love when we feel most unloved.

A few words about the subtitle of the book—*Ministry, Madness, Mission.* The book was originally conceived as a series of devotions on Psalm verses, reflecting on living with this particular mental illness. An early working title was *From Sheol to the Highest Heavens: 101 Devotions for People with Bipolar Disorder (and those who love them).* As I worked through several drafts, I realized I needed to say more about my own journey – in faith as well as with a mental illness.

As part of a workshop on "Writing Your Spiritual Autobiography," I composed a narrative poem in ten parts (or seasons). This will serve as the "framework" for the "house" of my bipolar mind. It describes my call to

4

ministry, my descent into madness, and ends at the point where my mission begins—to share my story of how God led me to delight in the midst of my disorder.

Finally, my purpose in writing this book is principally to give glory to God for bringing me through this crazy life no matter how much of a mess I make of it. I pray that the sometimes profane details of my life don't cause you to stumble as you take the journey with me.

While I have written this devotional with an eye toward the millions who share my illness, my hope is that anyone who picks it up will find words of encouragement to delight in your disorder and meditate on the goodness of God in the land of the living.

Prelude: To Nineveh (and back)--
A Memoir of Faith and Madness

i. Out of Nineveh

When I was born, Nineveh was no longer the capital of an
evil Assyrian empire.
It was a small town in the Midwest, straight out of Hoosiers.
With a mother seeking comfort, finding passing victory in
Valium.
And a father consumed by work; entangled by emotions
unexpressed.
Their friends put beer in my bottle and laughed
At the toddler toddling tipsy to the turf.

A picture in the school yearbook shows me at age three.
In the crowd at a basketball game,
Eyes riveted on the action; not reacting like others;
Searching for substance in the orange globe of a ball
As if God put it there.

Sports structured my days,
A soothing, sure escape.
Countless hours at the school playground
As Pistol Pete Maravich.
Each shot a last-second buzzer beater,
A ticket to immortality.

When my parents divorced,
I was made to choose where to live.
I chose Dad's – where I could be free
To eat Braunsweiger and Nacho Cheese Doritos

Until I made myself sick.

Dad's buddies came over to drink Budweiser,
One asked, "Do you like playing with yourself?"
I said, "Sure."
He burst out laughing;
Spewing beer through his nose.

I moved in with Mom and Dan, my step-father.
He was an EMT and liked to carry guns.
We watched "Emergency" during dinner.
Dan yelled at the TV, shouting instructions.

They argued a lot – Mom and Dan.
One day, their yells reached a feverous pitch
their arms were raised.
I was struck by the image of a gun.

I felt a sharp stab in my gut and yelled out.
Dan looked at me
And decided my appendix had burst.
He rode with me in an ambulance to the hospital.
They diagnosed it as gastritis.

I believe it was the finger of God.

I was driven to succeed in high school
In sports and studies.
My senior year I discovered girls,
Paula in particular.
To date her, I had to go to church,
Which I gladly did.
She wanted more than kisses and cuddling.

I wanted more than her body had to offer.

At eighteen, I was on top of the world
But knew it was not a steady place to stand.
I had mono when I gave the graduation speech.
I talked about the need for faith,
With a runny nose.

I recited the poem "Richard Cory," which begins,

Whenever Richard Cory went down town,
We people on the pavement looked at him:
He was a gentleman from sole to crown,
Clean favored, and imperially slim.

And ends…

So on we worked, and waited for the light,
And went without the meat, and cursed the bread;
And Richard Cory, one calm summer night,
Went home and put a bullet through his head.[2]

ii. Higher Education

College was a place to experiment,
Mixing songs with sex, ideas with drugs.
The God I had come to know went up in smoke.
I replaced the living Word with words from lives
That thirsted for truths to absorb the Truth
And hungered for rights without Righteousness.

I wrote a book my senior year called,
Life (in obvious places)

Filled with family stories and ones I'd conceived.
At the end, a coquettish Claudia Matson asks the narrator,
"Why don't you write any love stories?"
"I don't know any," he replies.

I took a job at a plastics factory
And started going to a country church—
Grammar Presbyterian.
Filled with farmers and grandmothers
Who made room for me in my stained Salvation Army
clothes
Smelling of smoke, looking for a God of substance.

Easter Sunday, on my way to church.
I saw a grey-haired woman in a tattered coat wandering.
I pulled over and tried to help.
She didn't know where she was.
I didn't know where to take her.
We were both lost.

I drove her to a church downtown.
Dressed in his Easter best, an usher gave her coffee and a
muffin.
He sat with her and helped her find her way home.
I left the church in tears.
Finding strength to be weak in a community of grace.

I went to seminary to serve God with my mind,
Hoping my body and soul would follow.
In class we looked at the language of Scripture
And discussed how not to talk about God.

In my pastoral work, I found God:

9

in the joy of a boy who would never speak.
in the songs of prisoners longing for freedom.
in the tears of a man praying beside his dying wife's bed.

I say I found God,
But really God found me,
I just didn't run away.

I met Alice in the office of friends.
She was arguing with the phone company about a deposit.
She won.
I said to myself, "I want her on my side."
Within six months, we were engaged.
We moved to a three-room row house in South St. Louis.
The heat was unbearable,
Steam rising from the asphalt.
We passionately loved and more passionately fought.
From this conjugal clash, a child was conceived.

We moved to the countryside,
And I became a pastor,
Shepherd of a frozen flock.
I delivered sermons on Sunday,
And took out the trash on Tuesdays.

Sarah Emily was born in early spring.
There was a chill in the air and ice on the roads,
But we barely noticed.
We brought her home to balloons and signs;
A Noah's Ark nursery.

We made her first week a music video
with Sandi Patty singing,

You are a masterpiece
A new creation He has formed
And you're as soft and fresh as a snowy winter morn.
And I'm so glad that God has given you to me.[3]

After a week, I was spent (or so I thought).
I retreated to my office and didn't come out
Even when I came home.

iii. Prayer, Parenting, Pits, and Pills

In a fit of creative energy, I composed a book on prayer.
I was so busy with prayer that I made no time to pray.

I started a book on faithful fathering;
Alice took Sarah to a friend's.
They were gone three days.
When they returned, I fell into a deep despair,
Sleeping days, staying up all night.

A friend recommended his psychiatrist,
Who prescribed pills—
A new generation of anti-depressants.
Not your mother's Valium, I was assured.

With prayer and pills, God and therapy,
I found some relief.

Released, we conceived again –
Our graceful pilgrim,
Grace Alehah.

Tony Roberts

iv. The Clarion Call

Our pilgrimage led East – to Pennsylvania.
I became pastor of a heavily-endowed church
Looking for an infusion of youthful zeal,
A young pastor to do the trick.

I was full of myself, but little else.
When growth was slow, I fell down in despair.
And looked to a new drug to pick me up.
Effexor did just that—
It picked me up and kept me up for six solid days and
nights.

Street signs became messages from God.
Ideas became revelations.
Feverous with a mission, not to assuage but to save,
I started crying during sermons
And laughing when I was alone.

Alice took me to Clarion hospital.
As they fastened the door,
I started pacing the floor.
Sensing some signal.

It was the end of the world.
I was in the only safe haven left.
I had to break out and bring my family back.

I grabbed a plate full of sugar cookies.
And shoved them in my mouth.
Then I took off running toward the glass door,
Crashing into it with a loud BANG.

A crowd gathered around me,
I shoved them away and started running for another door.
They surrounded me and thought they had me subdued.
(Or so they told me later.)

v. Alone in a Fog

I woke up in a solid white room.
Alone, strapped to a bed.

"You have bipolar disorder," they said.
I got a diagnostic code to replace
My points per game, my GPA, and my SAT score.
DSM 296.4x4.
I would need treatment the rest of my life.

I spent most of the next year heavily medicated.
I prayed to God, but couldn't hear a response.
I read the Bible, but the message escaped me.
I tried to write, but the words wouldn't come.
Mostly I slept, and ate, and took pills.

My mind was thick like fog.

One day Alice was taking a nap with the children.
A friend stopped by to take me for coffee
I left a note which read:

"Dear sugar bear,
Gone to the mountains to pick blueberries.
Be back by spring."

13

The church was wondrously generous.
They provided me paid leave.
They stopped by with meals.
They watched Sarah and Grace
When Alice and I had appointments.
Eventually, I went back to work full time.
But I had nothing left for home (or so I thought).

Alice was fed up.
She decided to get a job,
Then a divorce.
We went for counseling as a last resort.

In counseling, the fog started to lift.   — A process.
Not overnight, but gradually, and steadily.
I asked Alice to stay.
She agreed, thank God.

vi. On a Teeter-Totter

We enjoyed some time of basic balance.
Like when you're matched with someone of equal weight
On a teeter-totter.

But soon we learned that Alice's father had cancer.
Colon cancer – very aggressive.
She took the children and moved in with her mom to help.
He made it through surgery, but something went wrong
And he ended up in a coma.

For six weeks Alice managed her father's illness,
Advocating for him while caring for Sarah and Grace.
I came up on Sunday nights and stayed through Tuesdays,

14

The pastor's version of a weekend.

It was winter time, and the storms blew strong,
But we weathered them together, traveling the distance.

They discovered his chemo had induced the coma.
With time and physical therapy, he got better.
Alice and the girls returned home,
Eager for spring, looking for new life.

Alice wanted more children.
It was her calling, to be a mom.
We became foster parents.
Shortly after being approved, we got a call.
Two sisters, ages five and nine, needed a place to stay.
Jessie and Elena became part of our family.
They were with us over a year before
They found a permanent home.

Life was good.
God was in heaven, and all seemed right with the world.
But I longed for more.

vii. In the Heart of the Finger Lakes

I heard of a church in upstate New York
Searching for a pastor.
It was just two towns over from Alice's parents.
I wasn't looking to leave, but the location seemed perfect.
We went through the process and a call was confirmed.

Ovid rests between the two largest fingers of the Finger
Lakes.

Tony Roberts

If you climb the church steeple, you can see
Cayuga Lake to the north and
Seneca Lake to the west.

I was the only pastor in town,
So I became the village vicar.
We ran a Thrift Shop where you could get any item of clothing
For less than a buck.
We housed the Food Pantry where you could get a week's worth of groceries
For free.

People came for prayer and stayed for service.
I led a twelve-step Bible study group at a local addiction treatment center.
I cheered on the basketball teams,
And went to the school plays.

My devotion to ministry fueled
My commitment as a father.
We homeschooled Sarah and Grace.
I kept the shelves stocked
With the best books I could find.
We wrote our own stories, went camping,
Danced in the park.

My journals from our Ovid years show shortcomings,
Spiritual and relational struggles that kept it from being
Paradise on earth.
But when God created the earth, He didn't call it great.
He called it good. And then He rested.

3. of high quality; excellent
4. right; proper; fit
16. favorable; propitious; indicating a good chance
    of success
2. satisfactory in quality, quantity or degree

viii. Chosen to Adopt

While at Ovid,
We were blessed to be a blessing.
Inspired by a book called *Expecting Adam*
We chose to adopt a child with Down syndrome.

Within a few months,
We got a call from an agency in Albany
For an eight-week old boy we named
Caleb Ezra Anthony.

The church adored Caleb,
Lavishing him with affection.
He would raise his hands in praise,
And direct the people to sing with joy.

In time, we chose to be chosen again.
We flew to New Orleans for our BUFA girl –
Baby Up For Adoption, we named
Hannah Elizabeth Sarai.
Our ugly duckling soon became
A beautiful swan.

ix. Lost on Long Island

In high school, I learned the Peter Principle,
"People rise to their level of incompetence."
In seminary, I was taught,
"Be careful what you pray for;
You might just get it."
Still, I prayed to rise,
More people, a bigger community, better pay.

17

A church on Long Island called
And offered me all this and more –
      more than I expected.
      more than I could handle.

From the moment I landed, I was consumed with busyness
That had no end.
The church needed a Savior.
And I wasn't Him.
The ministry became my golden calf
Where I sacrificed my family and my sanity.

One night I went to bed early,
Emotionally exhausted and physically drained.
Lying in bed, I heard a voice say, "It's okay."

But it wasn't the voice of assurance.
It was a word of relinquishment.

I got up and filled my palm with psychotropic drugs.
Put them in my mouth and swallowed.
I did it again. And again.

It wasn't enough to kill me.
Only to put me in a drug-induced stupor.
I collapsed on the floor.

Alice found me and called my psychiatrist
He said I could sleep it off.
But I kept falling onto the floor.
My body was contorted; I kept running into walls.
Alice had to direct me to the bathroom,

And clean up after me when I missed.

I was angry –
angry at myself for making such a mess of things.
angry at Alice for cleaning up my mess.
angry at God for messing with me.

x. Back to Nineveh

Some people ask me now how someone who claims
To have a saving relationship with Jesus Christ
Could try to kill himself.

My only answer is –
Though I've wanted to give up on God,
God hasn't given up on me.

Now I've come back to the outskirts of Nineveh,
I'm hiding from the scorching sun,
Grateful for the shade God provides.

1. The Front Porch

My heart lies at Your feet in fear.
My vision trembles and thoughts cry:
Shall He that made the ear not hear?

I wait through all the waiting year,
Bringing You my waning sigh;
My heart lies at Your feet in fear

And yet this quiet hope hangs near,
A question with no firm reply:
Shall He that made the ear not hear?

I watch, in hope You will appear;
Lord, hear! I cry. My words aim high –
My heart lies at Your feet in fear.

Clouds laugh at me and vacuums jeer;
But there is time still to defy.
Shall He that made the ear not hear?

The heavens sit, a blank frontier,
Yet nothing hides there from Your eye.
My heart lies at Your feet in fear...
Shall He that made the ear not hear?[4]

~ "He that made the ear" by Matthew Pullar (After George Herbert's "Longing")

Our family home rests on a plot of seven and a half acres in the Finger Lakes region of upstate New York. One of the features we fell in love with when we found the house is the large front porch.

We moved in during March – mud season. We quickly fell into the habit of removing our shoes on the porch so as to not track in a mess. When we found the floor to be a little chilly in socked-feet, we placed slippers just inside the front door to put on as we entered.

We remove our shoes for purely pragmatic reasons. We don't have any cultural or religious mandates. We don't have any safety concerns (like when I've had to remove my shoes at psychiatric units so I wouldn't hang myself with the shoelaces). We do it purely to keep the house clean. And we provide slippers for comfort.

I've placed the meditations in this section on "the front porch" because they offer views of faith and mental illness that help you remove the mud-caked stereotypes of the world before you enter into the particular perspective I have as a person of faith with a mental illness. While the "slippers" I provide may seem foreign and fail to fit perfectly, hopefully they will keep your feet warm as we explore the house together.

Tony Roberts

Sin and Sickness

*Look on my affliction and my distress
and take away all my sins.* (Psalm 25:18) See 16-18 also

Over the years, I've given a lot of thought to the relationship between sin and sickness. The Bible clearly connects the two, but it is not always clear exactly what the relationship is.

There are times when sickness is caused by what someone does or fails to do – as when the foolish Nabal's inhospitable demeanor leads to a heart attack (1 Samuel 25).

Other times, sickness is not caused by a person's sin but rather is a test of righteousness, such as when Satan tests Job.

Sickness can result from

- the transmission of sin (generational sin or a genetic flaw).

- the commission of sin (rebelling against God's commands or making unhealthy choices).

The relationship between sin and sickness can become particularly controversial when it comes to mental illness. Over the years, people have been taught that mental illness is demon possession either invited in or allowed to remain in a person's life through some lingering sin. To counteract this stigma, many modern people abandon the connection between sin and sickness altogether.

I see my bipolar illness as the result of generational sin. This does not pin the blame either on my parents or any particular ancestor. It does, however, recognize what both the Bible says and what science has found to be true. Something is not right within me and it is not something I created. It has been passed down for generations.

22

Sin and sickness are related. Unless we see this in our lives, we may fail to take advantage of opportunities to experience healing. Had the paralytic man quibbled with Jesus about his sin when Jesus pronounced forgiveness, he might not have been healed (see Matthew 9). We need to both seek treatment for the "genetic component" to our illness as well as recognize our part in aggravating our symptoms (and make changes).

This is just as true for persons with bipolar as for those with physical conditions such as diabetes, heart disease, or obesity. We need to ask ourselves,

"Am I receiving the best treatment available?"
"Am I taking the prescribed meds?"
"Am I seeking spiritual help?"

If the answer to any of these is *"No,"* chances are we don't really want to be healed. If, however, we can confidently answer, *"Yes"* to these questions, we are no doubt looking to the Lord for healing and will receive it in good time – maybe not according to our desires, but definitely according to our needs.

Tony Roberts

Even Me

But you, God, see the trouble of the afflicted;
you consider their grief and take it in hand.
The victims commit themselves to you;
you are the helper of the fatherless. (Psalm 10:14)

I learned growing up the importance of being in a personal relationship with Jesus Christ. I was taught to maintain this relationship with daily prayer and Bible reading, weekly worship, and regular fellowship with Christians. In spite of this, I often pulled away, turning inward in times of trouble, becoming reclusive when my feelings and beliefs didn't line up. I believed I was made to praise God with my whole heart, mind, and being. Yet, my feelings were far from God, and I instead obsessed about all that was wrong with me and with the world.

Over the past several years now, I've often wondered how I could be in a personal relationship with the LORD and still have tried to take my life. Attempting suicide, while often prompted by disturbed minds (like mine), is an ultimate act of ingratitude for the life God has given us. Yet, after my attempt, I felt drawn closer to God more than ever. Perhaps out of desperation. More likely out of desire.

Some talk about the "assurance of salvation" – once saved, always saved. Others point to Bible passages that show it is possible to "fall from grace." I've thought hard and prayed deep about the subject and have yet to come to any conclusions. I can only say that, in my life, while there have been plenty of times I've felt like giving up on God, God has never given up on me.

I don't always *feel* secure in my salvation, but I do *know* the power of Christ's saving love first-hand in my life.

24

God has brought me back from the dead. In Christ, I have hope for abundant life with him now and forever.

The Psalmists show us that those who look to the LORD for salvation experience how intimately God is connected to us. God sees our troubles even before they are troubles. God knows our grief and grieves with us. When we feel the most helpless, we can turn to the LORD and be swept up in God's warm embrace.

When I came to my senses in the hospital bed after my suicide attempt, I had to face the reality that I had tried to abandon God. At the same time, I discovered God had not abandoned me. I say this not to brag about my standing with God – indeed I have no standing with God. I say this instead with tremendous gratitude and wonder that God would take notice of me—even me.

Tony Roberts

The Healing Power of the Psalms

LORD my God, I called to you for help,
and you healed me. (Psalm 30:2) also 3

People like to display their family Bibles when the pastor comes to visit. On one such visit in my first pastorate, my hosts opened up their Bible and showed me a unique treasure I'd not seen before or found since. Written in the margins of the Psalms were folk remedies detailing how one could find healing. The instructions were very specific –

"Say this Psalm five times for sore throat."
"Good for gout."
"Heals dizziness."

At first I smiled at the gross superstition of those who applied Scripture in such an ignorant manner. Over the years I've come to appreciate, instead, how simply profound their faith may well have been. It takes courage to trust that the God who created heaven and earth takes pains even to heal my headaches.

Healing happens. Can you believe it? If you find yourself ill reading this book, read on. You may find, as I have, healing waters coming through the Psalms in drips and drabs as well as in overflowing floods. Healing comes to those who, like me, suffer with a serious mental illness and to those who battle morning sickness. Healing comes even (perhaps especially) to those facing pain as they near life's end. It may not be precisely the healing we ask for, but it is just the healing we need – a healing that brings glory to God and draws us closer to Christ.

No matter our pain – physical, emotional, spiritual – God wants to make us well.

26

This is the great Good News. Can you believe it?

Escaping the Pain

In the LORD I take refuge.
How then can you say to me:
"Flee like a bird to your mountain"? (Psalm 11:1)

When I first began to experience the symptoms of bipolar, I tried to escape them with drugs and alcohol, what some call self-medicating. As you might expect, this only made things worse. Treating a mood disorder with non-prescribed mind-altering drugs is not something I would now recommend.

I then tried to treat my symptoms with only talk therapy and self-help techniques. While it was good to get off un-prescribed drugs, talk therapy alone was ultimately ineffective. It wound up being another form of escapism from my full problem. It was bipolar disorder causing a chemical reaction in my brain, and I needed something more than encouraging words to re-establish balance.

One thing I've discovered in my journey through bipolar is that faith and medicine can, and often do, work well together as partners to promote healing. We find refuge in the Lord when we resist our urge to "flee like a bird to your mountain," and instead seek professional help and spiritual guidance.

The combination of talk and drug therapy has worked well for me over the course of my illness. Counseling goes a long way to help me sort out my mind and function better when the right dosages of medication are balancing the chemicals in my brain. Properly prescribed medication takes enough of the edge off my pain such that I can be more productive in my therapeutic work.

There is no way to escape the pain we are bound to feel

28

as we battle bipolar or other serious illnesses. Yet, we can find refuge in the LORD if we avoid the damaging flight of escape and face our suffering with all the spiritual and medical resources God provides.

ie - Self medicating
- dosing myself down because I "feel good"
- locking myself away when depressed
- Blaming others for my pain & noncompliance to helpful strategies.

Tony Roberts

Out of the Depths

Out of the depths I cry to you, LORD;
Lord, hear my voice.
Let your ears be attentive
to my cry for mercy.

If you, LORD, kept a record of sins,
Lord, who could stand?
But with you there is forgiveness,
so that we can, with reverence, serve you. (Psalm 130:1-4)

♡ this whole Psalm

When I am in the grip of depression, the last thing I want to hear is that I've done nothing to deserve it. My mind busily rehashes old regrets. I am convinced of my guilt over many things. I see my depression – no matter how severe – as but a small price to pay for my sin.

The good news that saves us from the darkest corners of depression is not that we are "good enough" on our own. It is that in spite of how horribly we mess up, God has a word of grace to speak to us. God will lift us up when we have fallen into a pit. We don't have to be "good enough" for grace.

God's is not the hounding voice of the depression – pointing out to us every flaw, every mistake, and every fault. God's is the Voice of the father who joyfully tells his servants to "kill the fatted calf" when his son returns home.

God's is the still small Voice gently reminding us whose we are and telling us what we can do to make things better.

God's is the Voice who calls out to all created things, "You are good." – See def of Good pg 16

God's is the Voice that spoke from the heavens at the baptism of Jesus, "You are my Son, with you I am well

30

pleased."

The Voice of God answers our own meager voices crying out in such a way that we know we are heard and loved.

Tony Roberts

Scorn-full

Have mercy upon us, O Lord, have mercy upon us,
for we have had more than enough of contempt.
Our soul has had more than its fill
of the scorn of those who are at ease,
of the contempt of the proud. (Psalm 123:3-4)

While modern medicine has come a long way in helping us understand and explain mental illness, people's perspectives can lag far behind. Many people still think that with more faith, a stronger will, and a better attitude, such things as depression, bipolar disorder, even schizophrenia can just go away.

This outlook often leads to pinning the blame for the illness on the person struggling to overcome it. It can also lead to contempt and scorn on the part of the accuser that the accused may internalized. → typo?

"If you only had more faith."
"If you weren't so lazy."
"If you just kept a positive attitude."

Like the Psalmist, I have had more than my fill of contempt from people lacking understanding and compassion. From the colleague who advises me to *"Just get more exercise,"* to the church leader who quietly slips a stack of positive thinking pamphlets on my desk. From the well-meaning friend who tells me to *"Take it to the Lord in prayer,"* (as if I haven't), to the recreational therapist who insists I dance the Macarena. All these things might be helpful in themselves, but none of them can remove my illness and often they reveal an underlying sense of contempt that I'm not doing enough to alleviate my struggle.

32

I cansoooo relate!

While I don't usually dispense advice, some advice to those of you who have loved ones with a mental illness – "Don't give advice." It is often thinly-veiled contempt for someone you fail to understand and appreciate as an authentic person whose struggle is far deeper than any pious platitude can go.

If you are looking for an appropriate way to respond to a person struggling with a mental illness, look to Job's friends. Not when they made the mistake of opening their mouths to try to explain his suffering, but when they first arrived and simply sat with him in silence.

One thing my wife and children learned to do well when I was going through hard times is to offer me the blessing of their presence, without trying to cheer me up or blame me for being down. As difficult as this was for them to do, it was a great help for me when I could see that my mood disorder could be somewhat contained within me – and not overly impact the mood or behavior of those I loved.

Their commitment to go about life around me also showed that they trusted my ability to battle my bipolar, with God's help, and that as I was able to come back around, they would be there for me. Instead of being full of scorn, they showed me great respect.

Escape from Death

Our God is a God who saves;
from the Sovereign LORD comes escape from death. (Psalm
68:20)

In the years since my suicide attempt I've had a great
deal of time to reflect on its meaning and the purpose of my
life then and now. At times, I've described it as a one-time
fluke. I had never before nor have I since been seriously
suicidal. But the attempt was more than a fluke. It was an
attack.

It was a spiritual attack from an enemy who wants
nothing more than to get God's children to give up. It was
an attack for which I was ill-prepared despite decades of
study and devotion. It was an attack I pray never comes
again though I know it could. I know I need to be
devotionally disciplined on a daily basis in case I am
attacked again.

The most important part of the story of my suicide
attempt is not what happened before I took the pills, but
afterward. I managed to escape death thanks to God, the
God of my salvation.

This is the part of the story I need to always remember
and tell others. I faced death and, by the grace of God, have
lived to tell about it.

Even as I write this, I realize that not everyone is
rescued, at least in this life. I think of Matthew Warren who,
only a week ago today, took his own life. I think of
something his father Rick said – even on that day Matthew
was playing family games and having a good time.

It is true that some people with mental illnesses don't
survive deathly attacks. I can't make sense of it, but I do

believe God is still our salvation, that God has a saving purpose for all His children. Mental illness is a mystery we may never solve, not a puzzle we can piece together.

The best we can do is look to the Lord – who is our rock and our salvation, our best and only hope – in this life and beyond. In Jesus Christ, God brings us back from the grave. We escape the death that is the sure sentence of our sin to enjoy life with Christ and with all God's children forever.

Tony Roberts

A Horror Story

You have taken from me my closest friends
and have made me repulsive to them.
I am confined and cannot escape;
my eyes are dim with grief.
I call to you, LORD, every day;
I spread out my hands to you. (Psalm 88:8-9a)

You have taken my companions and my loved ones from me;
the darkness is my closest friend. (Psalm 88:19)

For the most part, I have been very blessed when it comes to family and friends responding to my illness. My wife stayed with me for over 20 years, and while we are now separated geographically, we are still united in marriage, and she still communicates with care. My mother and father and their spouses have supported me. My sister and brother-in-law have been wonderful. Others have stayed in touch. The few friends and family members who have grown distant over the years may well have done so due to reasons other than diagnosis.

I have seen cases, however, where mental illness takes a severe toll on relationships. I had companions in the psychiatric units where I've stayed who had no visitors, received no mail, and got no phone calls. Often, this sent them further into seclusion and contributed to a bitterness that only turned more people away—a vicious cycle.

I wouldn't pin the blame on God for causing such things to happen, but it's natural to wonder. It does seem that when one person becomes ill, people rally around her/him (as in my case). Meanwhile, when it happens to someone else, s/he is left alone. It hardly seems fair.

36

Why is it that some, like the Psalmist here, wind up with darkness as their closest friend?

The best I can provide is more a theological answer than a pastoral one (which may be totally unsatisfactory for a person in the darkness). It may be that God sometimes removes relationships from us (or creates distance) so that we would grow closer in our relationship with Him. The darker our loneliness gets, the more we are likely to reach out to the One who is already in pursuit of us.

How exquisitely TRUE

A Quick Prayer

Hear my prayer, LORD;
let my cry for help come to you.
Do not hide your face from me
when I am in distress.
Turn your ear to me;
when I call, answer me quickly. (Psalm 102:1-2)

I believe in miracles. Some miracles happen immediately while others take time. Miracles don't necessarily take the shape we most desire. In some ways the Bible does us a disservice showing only those times when Jesus successfully (and instantaneously) performed miracles. There is only one verse (Matthew 13:58) that refers to a time when miracles were not performed in Christ's healing ministry.

I would like nothing better than to wave a magic prayer wand and have my bipolar disorder magically disappear – speedily. But after a life-long struggle with the illness, I don't believe this is going to happen. Maybe I lack faith, but I think it's something more. I think God has a plan for me to have this illness and function in spite of it. *Me too!*

I have a good friend from high school who also battles bipolar. Like me, he has a foundation of faith that helps him manage from day to day. Recently, though, some family members and friends have been inflicting on him a steady stream of "name it, claim it" messages from a "health and wealth" theology. This movement takes specific passages from Scripture out of context and contends that God desires everyone to be physically healthy.

This theology is a serious misrepresentation of the Gospel. It does much more damage than good. Certainly, we should pray for healing and eagerly await God's response, but God's idea of healing is often quite different from our own. God's primary interest is not to alleviate our suffering, but to lead us toward abundant life – no matter how painful it is to get there.

My prayer, my cry to the LORD is not to remove my illness, but to give me purpose and direction in the midst of it.

exactly!

2. The Family Room

Abiram, swallowed up by earth, was taken
Into the fiery core, our spinning planet
Not pausing to release him from its vortex;
I too am drawn in.

The Potter's Field received Judas' silver,
His body taken into soil, the true cost
Of what he bought Caiaphas with a swift kiss
From betraying lips.

I would have taken less than thirty pieces;
I have betrayed my Saviour for a trinket.
So I, like Judas and like dead Abiram,
Deserve gravity.

There is no soil to bury my betrayal
Or hide the bones that I have stripped of all flesh.
Only the night can for a time disguise them,
Soon to be found out.

Bright light – only when You enter my insides
Can darkness' strong pull on me be halted.
Only if You come swiftly with Your promise
Will the vortex stop.[5]

~ Buried Above Ground by Matthew Pullar (After William
Cowper's "Lines Written During a Period of Insanity")

We've exchanged greetings on the front porch. You've
taken off your mud-caked shoes and placed some slippers
on your feet. Now, I'd like you to follow me to the left, into

40

(handwritten, vertical left margin:) Amazing Poem which I completely agree + relate with

the family room.

There are wide-planked wooden floors marked up more than a bit from when we've moved furniture around. The furniture has been handed down from generation to generation, some of it refurbished, some of it worn and tattered from family cats before we had them de-clawed. There are quilts made from old clothing and an afghan crocheted with prayer while awaiting news from one of my hospitalizations. The walls are filled with family pictures from cross-country trips to daily activities, like building snowmen and feeding the goats. Biblical verses and spiritual mottos are framed beside the photos, reminding us of our purpose and identity.

We sit down, get comfortable and talk about common things that reveal who we are, who we've been, and to Whom we belong. We share family stories – some funny, some tragic – not as a way to brag about our pedigree (as if we had one), but to praise God from one generation to the next.

Genetic Predisposition

Do not hold against us the sins of past generations;
may your mercy come quickly to meet us,
for we are in desperate need. (Psalm 79:8)

While there may well be points of dispute in various areas, the Bible and modern science agree on one thing for sure. We inherit aspects of our being from our ancestors. Whether we call these things "iniquities" or "genetic markings," the point of the matter is, our mothers and fathers and those who make up our biological family in the past shape who we are in the present and influence who we become in the future.

As I've sought treatment for mental illness, I've come to discover I share the affliction with various ancestors and relatives. I try to put this knowledge in perspective and not let it drag me into the terrible trap of genetic determinism. Yes, I have a serious mental illness like other family members. But no, my life doesn't have to progress (or tragically end) as theirs did.

The prayer of this Psalmist is mine as I look back at my ancestry and look forward to the lives of my children. I pray the compassion of God would come speedily and lift me up when I am brought low reflecting on what has gone wrong in the past or what could go wrong in the future.

I pray the sin that has come to me from "the third and fourth generation" would be redeemed by Christ such that righteousness might reign in my children and my children's children "for a thousand generations to come." This may not mean their mental illness DNA is magically removed, but with better understanding, careful treatment, and intensive prayer, they would receive a degree of healing and recovery even beyond what I have experienced – without sinking into the dangerous depths or swinging to the deceptive highs that have marked my life.

What an awesome thought to pray about to Jesus for my girls + future generations!

Tony Roberts

Dust in the Wind

Lord, you have been our dwelling place
throughout all generations.
Before the mountains were born
or you brought forth the whole world,
from everlasting to everlasting you are God.
You turn people back to dust,
saying, "Return to dust, you mortals."
A thousand years in your sight
are like a day that has just gone by,
or like a watch in the night. (Psalm 90:1-4)

My grandfather, Joe Etsy, had a very rough start in life. His mother, Jeretta, died of tuberculosis when he was barely three months old. He was farmed out to his Uncle Ed and Aunt Toad, as his father Grover was in no condition to raise an infant. Ed and Toad did their best to raise Joe Etsy well, but he soon became a wanderer. At age 15, his eyes wandered to his cousin, Bessie, then 13. His feet followed and he eloped with her.

Though he fathered eight children, he wasn't much satisfied with domestic life. He was always looking for something more. The family moved to Indiana and lived for a while on a sizeable farm in Martinsville, picking acres of tomatoes, corn, and beans. Joe Etsy supplemented the family income with a factory job at Arvin's.

But the job didn't last. My dad thinks he was fired for trying to start a union. Joe Etsy claimed he quit. Whatever happened, he lost the steady income stream and the family moved to a farm tenant's shack in Franklin where they barely eeked out a living.

Joe Etsy came up with a grand scheme to earn money.

He bought an old school bus, painted it John Deere green and converted it into a sort of antique-mobile. He would drive "down home" to Kentucky and load it up with cheaply purchased goods to sell for a tidy profit up North. I once asked Dad if Joe Etsy made any money on the venture and he replied, "*If he did, the family didn't see any of it.*"

Something strange happened to Joe Etsy in his forties. He started to have violent seizures, experience radical mood swings, and display erratic behavior. Sometimes he would disappear for days, even weeks. When he was home, he would spend his days and nights in the coal shack, coming in for meals, hands all blackened. After eating, he would take a piece of bread and roll it in his hands until it was black as coal.

One night in a blinding snow, Grandma Bessie and Joe Etsy had a terrible argument. He wanted to walk over a mile up the road to get some cigarettes. She tried to convince him to stay. He finally relented and told her to go inside, that he would be in soon.

After some time passed, Bessie got worried. She asked her young son, my uncle Larry, to check on his dad in the coal shack. Larry went out and called for his father. No response.

Then he looked down the road. In the distance he could see in the headlights of a pick-up truck a body lying on the ground.

Joe Etsy had been out wandering again. In a blinding storm. In the middle of the road. His wandering days were over.

Tony Roberts

Trust in God

*Whoever dwells in the shelter of the Most High
will rest in the shadow of the Almighty.
I will say of the LORD, "He is my refuge and my fortress,
my God, in whom I trust." (Psalm 91:1-2)*

They say there are no atheists in foxholes. I wouldn't know about that, but I do know that the more time I have spent taking shelter from spiritual and emotional attack, the more I have come to rely on the LORD.

The nights I spent listening to my parents scream at each other over the events of the day through the thin walls of my boyhood home.

The days I saw my grandfather slapping kids around on the school bus for perceived disobedience, wondering if I might be next.

The Sundays in church when it seemed as if the hellfire and brimstone would fall on us as we sat still on those hardwood pews.

The weeks, months, and years I have spent fearful I would lose everything as I lost my mind, my memory, and my reason to live.

Over the years, I've learned to take shelter in the Most High. My biggest trouble has been coming out of hiding, trusting that God will lead me the rest of my days. If you, like me, have trouble coming out of hiding, take heart in these verses (above) and know you have a God you can trust who will never leave you and cannot forsake you.

I have learned in my years seeking shelter that God is always there to protect us even when it seems horrible things are going to happen. God cares for us even when all else turns against us. When family members abandon us.

46

When enemies abuse us. When friends reject us.

When my parents divorced, I lost all faith that any human relationship could last a lifetime. Sixteen years later, as I tried to profess my own wedding vows, I became choked up. The pastor, who couldn't see my face tried to feed me the words, thinking I had forgotten them— "I, Tony, take you, Alice... I, Tony, take you, Alice."

But I was having no problem with my memory. In fact, I was remembering well the many days I spent as a young boy wondering if it were ever possible that I might share my life with someone "as long as we both shall live." In this moment, before God and many witnesses, I burst into tears, realizing that I was graced with the hope that what was humanly impossible was actually happening in my life by God's grace.

Over two decades later, I am still grateful for the One who is my shelter in the storms, my fortress when I am under enemy attack.

From My Mother's Womb

For you have been my hope, Sovereign LORD,
my confidence since my youth.
From birth I have relied on you;
you brought me forth from my mother's womb.
I will ever praise you. (Psalm 71:5-6)

While I may not have had an ideal upbringing, faith was certainly a key component in my life from before birth. I have many people to thank for this, including my mother. Also her mother (my Grandma McPeak), who would often read Bible stories to us grandchildren from a big hardcover picture book.

My sister April and I would go to church with our grandparents and Uncle Geoff. We would sit in the back seat and talk about the things we saw outside the window. The first one to see the church would holler – "I first it." The other would say, "I second it." On and on until someone said, "I ate it!" Then we would laugh outrageously at the concept of eating a church.

The church where we worshiped was called First Mt. Pleasant Baptist. They placed a premium on fiery preaching from the King James Bible. They had an extended altar call for sinners to repent (while the congregation sang "Just As I Am"). People came forward to receive Christ and be born again. Evidently, they had a notion that the "age of accountability" was around first grade, because that's when both my sister and I came forward – responding more to a fear of going to Hell than with faith in the grace of God through Christ.

Yet, I am grateful for my faith upbringing. I was able to develop daily disciplines of prayer and Scripture reading.

More importantly, I cultivated the value of having a relationship with Jesus Christ that provided me a solid anchor of hope as the world collapsed around me.

Not everyone is born into a family of faith, but the promise of these Psalm verses is that God takes us from our mother's wombs. While it helps to have a faith heritage, there is no "grandfather clause" in our covenant with God. Each of us is invited into a personal relationship with Christ that lights the ways through dark valleys and inspires us to offer up praise throughout our days.

Tony Roberts

A Father's Compassion

As a father has compassion on his children,
so the LORD has compassion on those who fear him;
for he knows how we are formed,
he remembers that we are dust. (Psalm 103:13-14)

In many ways, I am fortunate to come from the family I do. We may be crazy, but there is very little cruelty and, in many places, a generous portion of kindness toward each other as well as great compassion for others.

My father, for instance, is a very understanding man. He is the antithesis of those fathers who constantly place exceeding demands on their children (especially sons). Though I was a scholarship student, my father did not put too much pressure on me to excel.

One morning, before I left for college, he took me out for breakfast and encouraged me with these words, *"Tony, if you could just get C's, that would be great!"*

God does not expect more from us than we can achieve. God knows everything about us and has compassion for our weaknesses. As persons with Bipolar, God knows we have limitations, and knows our boundaries better than we do. God never expects us to go beyond what we are capable of doing. To paraphrase a Rabbinic saying,

"When I get to heaven, God will not ask me why I was not more like Moses. God will ask me why I was not more like Tony Roberts."

One of the best images of God's character in all of Scripture is in Luke 15, the "Parable of the Prodigal Son." I like how Timothy Keller reframes the parable and explores the "prodigal" nature of the father's love – extravagant, seemingly limitless, abundantly compassionate.[6]

50

The father loves both sons in the story. First, he notices his "lost son" in the distance. He hikes up his robe and runs out to welcome him home. He throws a party to celebrate the family reunion. Then, when he discovers his "steadfast son" missing from the party, he leaves behind the revelers to seek him out in the darkness of the older son's anger. The father assures this son of his constant love.

Like this father, God's compassion reaches out to us wherever we are. God reminds us Whose we are. God welcome us in from the cold, hard world. God breaks open our cold, hard hearts. We are warmed by the fire of God's compassionate love.

Tony Roberts

Dawn

Light shines on the righteous
and joy on the upright in heart. (Psalm 97:11)

In spite of dark moods I have felt from of depression, glimpses of light have flashed to help me see I am on the right track, in right relationships, making the right decisions. These moments have been accompanied with joy knowing I am not alone, and that my suffering is not in vain.

One such period of joy came when I first met Alice – the woman who would become my wife. I had been through a rough stretch and endured some painful relationships. I had nearly given up on finding a life companion. Lost in the darkness, I wrestled with the decision of whether to pursue an internship and devote myself solely to my pastoral career or continue working in group therapy on some pivotal issues that were hindering me from experiencing intimacy in relationships.

In the midst of darkness, a ray of light shone, and it dawned on me it would be best to stay and work through my relationship issues. That week, I met Alice and we began our life together. I cannot imagine I would have survived, much less thrived at times, in this journey without her.

Light dawns on us when we least expect it, when we most need it. It comes not just because we've done something right. Light shines because Jesus Christ has made things right through his sacrifice on the cross. The Righteous One directs his light on our darkness, brings clarity that speaks to our confusion and offers joy that brings laughter to our despair.

52

A Broad Place

When hard pressed, I cried to the LORD;
he brought me into a spacious place. (Psalm 118:5)

Before the birth of our first child, Sarah, I was battling a rough patch of depression. I was in a new pastorate and unsure of myself. Though God always provided, we had very little to live on. I was excited about becoming a father but also fearful about what kind of father I would be. I like to think I provided Alice the support she needed to have a reasonably enjoyable pregnancy, but I'm sure there were many days she wondered how I would function as a father and just how this whole marriage thing was going to work.

I turned to the LORD in some intensive prayer, asking for help to prepare for this major life change. I began to journal again, particularly on the Psalms. Not only did I lift up prayers, but I listened expectantly for God to respond. I could sense myself growing closer to the LORD, to Alice, and to this little baby growing within her.

By the time the baby arrived, it was as if God had set me in a "broad place" where I could function well. It's actually fun to watch the video of the hours right before and after Sarah's birth. I don't look like my usual sullen self or like some maniac bouncing off the walls. Alice has said I look just like "the man she most wanted to marry."

Prayer may not always be a magic panacea to cure all ills. It is, however, a lifeline we can draw on when we are in distress, when there is no place else to go. Rather than make it an occasional retreat, why not make it our first line of defense?

Led

He guided them with the cloud by day
and with light from the fire all night. (Psalm 78:14)

We need distinct things from God at each stage of our lives. God knows just what we need and provides it every step of the way.

The children of Israel needed a constant guide to make it through their wilderness wanderings and God provided one. Not only this, but God created it in a distinctive form they could best see – a billowy cloud by day and fiery cloud by night.

One night before Thanksgiving, our young family set out on a trip from Northeast Pennsylvania to the Finger Lakes region of New York to visit my Alice's parents. The forecast was calling for a snow storm and several church members tried to discourage us from travelling. But we were intent on going, and shortly after the Thanksgiving Eve service, we headed out.

My wife, who is more accustomed to driving winter roads, was in the driver's seat. Our two daughters cuddled up with blankets and pillows and fell asleep. I tried to stay awake to keep Alice focused, but I kept drifting off.

At one point, I tuned in and looked out the windshield. All I could see were the taillights of the semi in front of us.

"Don't you want to pull over?" I asked.

"I'm afraid to," Alice responded. *"I've been following the lights on this truck. It's all I've seen for over an hour. But we're going to need gas soon."*

As if on cue, the truck turned on his right signal to exit.

"I'm going to follow him," Alice said. *"Maybe he's stopping for gas."*

Sure enough, the semi pulled into a gas station. We filled up as well.

As we pulled out, we noticed the side of his truck. It said, "*Sure.*"

We laughed. That truck might have been filled with under-arm protection, but it was also God's sure way of protecting us and guiding us through the storm.

Tony Roberts

Inconsistency

Oh, that my ways were steadfast
in obeying your decrees! (Psalm 119:5)

One of my greatest frustrations living with bipolar disorder is how difficult it is to be consistent. This has caused me much anxiety and put tremendous strain on my relationships – particularly within my family. When I've felt up to it, I've made big plans to do things with the family, but then I crash and fail to follow through with them. When I've been depressed, I've let Alice make nearly all parenting decisions. Yet when I came back around, I've tried to assert my authority and made a mess of things.

At key moments I've been practically cruel in my inconsistency. One example was when we adopted our youngest child, Hannah. Alice wanted to provide her the nutritional and emotional benefits of nursing. Yet, I insisted this was selfish, that I should be included in the bonding experience of feeding her. Much to her dismay, Alice relented to my strong will. True to form, I didn't step up to the plate, and Alice wound up feeding Hannah from a bottle herself (with some help from our oldest daughters and grandparents).

Consistency is one of God's great character traits. When we become more like the LORD, we are bound to become more steadfast – particularly in our love. The ups and downs of our mood disorders don't go away, but they no longer command so much of our attention.

I like how we call what we do with faith, "practicing," The implication is we never fully perform it or perfect it in this life. The more we practice true faith, however, the more we consistently obey God's Word and Way.

56

I still have a long way to go when it comes to consistency. I'm still practicing what I believe is best, yet so often I fall short. When I do, I pray for forgiveness and pick up the next day and try again.

Tony Roberts

Joyful Noise

Make a joyful noise unto the LORD, *all the earth...* (Psalm 98:4a, KJV)

Having four children, I got to hear a great deal of noise – joyful and otherwise. I would like to say the noise was a blessing, and it was a blessing, of course, but too often I didn't experience it as such. While I realize any parent can grow weary of noise no matter how exuberant, I went through periods with my illness where almost any noise could be excruciatingly agitating. This made it difficult to share in many happy moments with my family as I sought out corners of dark silence to hide rather than join in the fun.

I don't know if this is specifically a feature of my illness or part of my character, but I greatly struggle with any noise that comes randomly, chaotically, spontaneously. I can listen to a familiar (sometimes rocking) song at top volume through my ear buds, but if I enter a room where there is loud conversation, laughter, and unfamiliar sounds, I soon become exhausted.

Though I rarely experience noise as a blessing, I did eventually learn to endure the sound (without much complaint) for the sake of the joy that comes when family members rejoice together. It has helped tremendously to have a wife so good at encouraging our children to delight in their discoveries of God's world and God's ways. This removed the pressure from me to be a "cheerleader." Instead, I became the quiet encourager who gently (and lovingly, I hope) helped them appreciate how joy comes in many forms, in all circumstances (no matter how much or how little noise we make).

Looking Up

I lift up my eyes to you,
to you who sit enthroned in heaven.
As the eyes of slaves look to the hand of their master,
as the eyes of a female slave look to the hand of her
mistress,
so our eyes look to the LORD our God,
till he shows us his mercy. (Psalm 123:1-2)

I remember a time in therapy when my counselor simply asked me to sit up straight and look at him. Somehow, the mere act of looking up was enough to lighten my load. There is something therapeutic about looking up, particularly when we look up as an act of reverence.

When I receive the blessing at the end of a worship service, I look up and breathe in the power of the Holy Spirit.

At a Billy Graham conference, I felt inspired as I looked up and joined countless others in songs of praise.

Driving around the Adirondacks near our family cabin, I look up and see the lofty mountains and am in awe.

As I awaken in the morning to my son's voice and looked up into his smiling face, I am reminded I have a reason to carry out the day.

At night I have looked up at my wife getting ready for bed and been grateful for the gift of her companionship.

Looking up to see the hand of the LORD in the works of creation can pick us up when we feel down or put us in our place when we are over-inflated with ourselves.

When we respond to life that often casts us down by looking up to God, things are simply bound to start looking up for us.

We are better able to face what lies ahead with confidence, assurance, and grace.

Majesty vs. Mania

When I consider your heavens,
the work of your fingers,
the moon and the stars,
which you have set in place,
what is mankind that you are mindful of them,
human beings that you care for them? (Psalm 8:3-4)

There have been some stages along my journey with bipolar when I've done rather well. We often tried to squeeze in something special for the family during these times. On one such occasion, we rented an RV and took a trip through various New England states, winding up in Maine at Acadia National Forest.

The scenery at Acadia is breath-taking. On a morning walk, I discovered a clearing in the woods. I did my devotionals sitting in the crag of some large stones while watching the sun rise over the mountain top. It was awe-inspiring. Wonderful. Humbling.

Unfortunately, this majestic setting was not able to keep my self-absorbed – and absorbing – mania from striking. I began to rapidly cycle. This put a serious damper on the trip. Still, nothing could take away from the beautiful creation we were able to experience. In spite of my radical mood swings, it was a vacation to remember.

God gives us amazing things to keep our hearts and minds looking outward, toward the LORD. Even when our Self gets in the way, God keeps calling us onward to see the beautiful sights ahead. The challenge is to resist the inward pull that tries to rob us of our appreciation for the ways of God, and to let go of all within us that distracts us from delighting in the LORD of all creation.

Being Led

The LORD is my shepherd; I shall not want.
He maketh me to lie down in green pastures:
he leadeth me beside the still waters. (Psalm 23:1-2, KJV)

To put it crassly, my family of origin was crazy. I dealt with the craziness by becoming a psychiatric patient. My sister dealt with it by becoming a psychiatric nurse. One of the programs she has worked for was known as a *Program for Assertive Community Treatment (PACT)*. Her job essentially entails getting people like me to do things that are good for them but that they'd rather not do. Things like:

• take medications regularly (even when they're enjoying a manic high).

• ask for help for services from people who are either annoyed by or afraid of them.

• get out in public when they'd much rather stay inside where they feel much safer.

Now, I don't want to suggest that my sister is God but, like God, she has to "shepherd" in such ways that soothe troubled spirits (*beside still waters*) and produce nourishing results (*lie down in green pastures*). As a person with bipolar, I know I can be a pretty stubborn sheep and, as the Psalmist later contends, I need the firmness of a rod and staff (metaphorically, if not physically) to bring comfort. Like God, my sister pursues people like me with "goodness and mercy" for as long as she can hoping and praying that they'll turn around and seek good health and well-being themselves.

Then and only then can we rest secure that we will "dwell in the house of the LORD forever." (Psalm 23:6)

When we internalize God's good law, when it is written in our hearts, we can function on a daily basis for our own good and for the glory of God.

Tony Roberts

Restoring Relationships

Create in me a pure heart, O God,
and renew a steadfast spirit within me. (Psalm 51:10)

At a Bipolar Support Group meeting I attended, a woman confessed to having repeated affairs on manic binges throughout her nine-year marriage. Once caught, she felt compelled to leave home, convinced after a particularly angry confrontation that her husband could never forgive her.

It is possible she was right. But I urged her to reconsider the decision to leave for good and at least work on their relationship. While infidelity does wreak havoc on many marriages, it is within God's power to purify our hearts stained with sin and renew our spirits so that love can be restored.

It doesn't always happen, but what a blessing it is when God claims victory over the forces that divide us and unites us once again. The statistics aren't good for persons with bipolar remaining married, but I have found tremendous reassurance having this sacred bond in my life to promote healing and wholeness.

Even now that I am separated from my wife and miss her daily companionship, I am still convinced of the permanent value of our vows and am grateful for her continued prayerful support. She is a wonderful mother for our children and a devoted "keeper at home." There have been times I have abused her trust, yet she has remained faithful. I pray, in the years ahead, I will show her as much steadfast love as she has shown me. And with God's help, I will.

3. The Living Room

The prince of love, he speaks in whispers,
whispers low to my heart's deep voice.
Where deep calls to deep
in waterfalls, I stand, his breakers
crashing down around me with
their silent shuddering, the voice
of love amidst the thundering;
to me he calls.

No-one there is with eyes of such fire
seated upon his sapphire throne,
with radiance that shines my soul with its burning
and his brightness a bow in a rainy-day's cloud.
Inexpressible, he is: how he blends such bright fury
with the gentlest whisper of his nail-scarred palms,
sparkling in glory over valleys,
the Son of Man.

Let the world have its dazzling allure and stories;
the eyes of this prince, this prince of love's glory
shine truer than all of the world's diamond lies.
He sits with the blind man and Zacchaeus, the road-side
his banqueting table, for Samaritans and me.
Sit with me, friends, at his morning-bright table
and we too will shine with him
eternally.[7]

~ "The Bright-Shining Lord" by Matthew Pullar (After Ann Griffith's "I Saw Him Standing")

In our house, there is a room just off the family room

we've used for various purposes. It has been a "music room" with a piano and CD player. It has been a "play room" with a toy box, monster Legos, and puzzles. It has served as a "sewing room," where Alice and our daughters have made dresses and pajamas and gathered with friends and family to create lovely quilts. It is also perfect as a "courting parlor," with a partition that separates it from the family room – providing just enough privacy and just enough connectedness.

In the house of my bipolar mind, the "living room" is the space where I meet people outside my family and find God at work in the world. Whether it be with church folks or fellow psychiatric patients, the elderly or the young, therapists or pastors, this is a space where I explore ideas beyond myself and examine my faith perspective to discover who I am and who I'm called to become.

I realize for many people who battle bipolar disorder, this is a room that can be unwelcoming, even frightening. This is just as true for church folks as well. We often prefer to "hang out" or "fellowship" with those who "get" where we are coming from, who share our "worldview." Yet, for spiritual and psychological growth to occur, we do best to follow the example of Jesus who ate with both publicans and Pharisees instead of hiding out in a hermitage.

Victory over Our Enemies

Listen to my cry,
for I am in desperate need;
rescue me from those who pursue me,
for they are too strong for me. (Psalm 142:6)

The greatest enemy I've faced in my disordered life has come from within – from the illness itself. The dangerous highs have skewed my perspective and taken my focus away from essential tasks I've needed to complete in order to be productive and lead a balanced life. The desperate lows have robbed me of the energy to do much of anything. Bipolar disorder has made a mockery of my mind and left my emotions ragged, strewn about like carcasses along life's road.

More than a few times, however, I have also had external persecution that seemed too strong to overcome. When I have "come out" about my illness, some people have become so disturbed that they've tried to prevent me from doing even what I do best. In a few cases, former friends have abandoned me and allies have betrayed me.

After several battles with such persecutors, I'm learning to let them be and accept that the path of non-resistance is most often the best path to take. I've seen ample evidence that their passion stems from unresolved issues over the illness in themselves or other loved ones. Nothing I can say or do will help them make them address this. I'm better off looking elsewhere for my support and being very selective about what battles I fight.

Persecutors can be very strong, as this Psalmist points out, but ultimately the power of the LORD prevails. We need to draw on God's strength each time we face persecution so that we can overcome.

There was one particular time in my ministry when I was under heavy attack. Unable to sleep, I walked through the darkness to church and entered the sanctuary. Circling the pews I started to pray, reciting –

Rescue me from those who pursue me,
for they are too strong for me!

My own tears mingled with the tears of the Psalmist, and for over an hour I cried out to God for relief. In time, I gained the strength to leave the sanctuary and re-enter the battle, confident God had heard me and would help me endure the attacks that came – with grace and love.

I look back on those days and marvel at how I functioned with a mental illness in such stressful situations. I certainly couldn't have done it alone. Thanks be to God, I didn't have to.

Desert Wastes

Some wandered in desert wastelands,
finding no way to a city where they could settle.
They were hungry and thirsty,
and their lives ebbed away.
Then they cried out to the LORD in their trouble,
and he delivered them from their distress. (Psalm 107:4-6)

I was fifteen years old when I first noticed a strange symptom that could have signaled my bipolar disorder. I was taking an Algebra test for which I was well prepared. I knew exactly how to solve the equations, yet there was a convicting "voice" inside me telling me I was stupid, that I was only fooling the world pretending to be a good student, and that I should just give up. The voice was so powerful, I had to ask to be excused for a drink to clear my mind. The voice then subsided somewhat, and I was able to score well on the test. But the experience is one I would never forget; one I would revisit in therapy many times as I explored the origin of the "voices" that have hounded me at various points throughout my life.

It took over fifteen more years of wandering in the desert waste of drug use (and abuse), mis-diagnosis, relational conflicts, and emotional crises before I was properly diagnosed. It then took another fifteen years to find the right chemical balance, treatment regiment, and spiritual discipline, to realize a period of "maintenance remission" – and I've only been able to experience this without the stress of a job (being on disability) and daily responsibilities as a husband and father (being separated from my family).

Thank God, though, I've not been alone in this desert waste. I have met many other wanderers (people wrestling with mental illness and other struggles). Just last week a man at church invited me to his home where a small group meets regularly for food, fellowship, Bible study and prayer. I shared some about my illness and this book project. He was eager that I meet a friend of his who had come to the group, yet was currently battling mental health issues and pulling away from the church. Later, I was asked to pray for this man and his family and for church members to have the wisdom and courage to reach out to them.

The delight in the disorder of bipolar is often found as we reach out to each other, as we connect with those who have similar struggles, as we share the faith and hope that keeps us going from day to day.

To a Spacious Place

Praise our God, all peoples,
let the sound of his praise be heard;
he has preserved our lives
and kept our feet from slipping.
For you, God, tested us;
you refined us like silver.
You brought us into prison
and laid burdens on our backs.
You let people ride over our heads;
we went through fire and water,
but you brought us to a place of abundance. (Psalm 66:8-12)

No matter what we have gone through—as people living with bipolar or people living with other limitations—we can rest assured that God is there for us. Here, the Psalmist encourages Israel to bless the God who has blessed them so much. Even though God tests and tries us, God ultimately gives us the strength to endure – to survive and eventually thrive in the midst of our trials.

If I could choose my medical profile, I would likely not opt to have bipolar. Yet, in the midst of my bipolar life, God has strengthened me such that I've come through it a better person. Through the intensity of my emotions, God has enabled me to better empathize with the hurts of humanity, to feel them in my gut, like the Bible says Jesus did with "bowels of compassion."

When I went back to pastoral ministry after my first diagnosis in 1995, people responded to me in various ways. There were some who kept me at arm's distance, perhaps concerned not to over-stress me, perhaps worried that my mental illness was contagious. Many others, however, reached out to me and confided in me their own battles with mental illness – either personally or in the lives of loved ones. Until then, they had kept quiet about it in church, not wanting others to know (fearful of how they would respond). I found them eager to unburden their hearts and minds through conversation and prayer about something they felt so deeply.

There was one older woman I visited who, as soon as I stepped through her door, challenged me with the statement, *"I thought Christians weren't supposed to get depressed."*

I smiled and took a deep breath. Then, I shared how some of the greatest Bible heroes went through terrible periods of depression. Moses prayed to be relieved of his duties as Israel's leader. Elijah wanted to end his life resting in the shade of a sycamore tree. David—a man after God's own heart—called out profusely to God to pay attention to his struggles. I opened my Bible and read a few passages in the Psalms where David cried out for emotional relief from God.

I saw a tear form in her eye, and she told me her story. She had battled crippling depression for years and had been told she was wrong to feel that way. Her challenging comment was not one that came from within her own heart. It was one imposed on her. It was something she had heard countless times from well-meaning, yet seriously misguided friends in faith.

Being Christians doesn't mean we never get depressed. It means we have Someone to turn to, who lifts the "crushing burdens on our backs," who leads us through fiery trials and floods of emotions to places of abundance where there is enduring joy and peace.

Where Is He?

Why, LORD, do you stand far off?
Why do you hide yourself in times of trouble? (Psalm 10:1)

When people in a psychiatric unit find out one of their own is a pastor, their behavior tends to change. Some clean up their language a good bit while others go out of their way to say something shocking. Some try to trip you up with trivial theological minutia while others seek you out as a spiritual guru.

I'll never forget the reception I once received from a young man named Daniel when he found out I was a pastor. Daniel had spiky hair and tattoos that covered his body. He came right up to me and said,

"Where is he?"

"Where is who?" I asked.

"God. Where is God?"

I paused and tried to determine if he was serious. He must have read my thoughts.

"I'm not trying to be a smart aleck. I really want to know. Is God somewhere in your life?"

Daniel then looked at me intently as I shared how God was with my wife when she found my body on the floor— dead weight from my attempted overdose. And with the psychiatrist who coached her through my admission to the hospital. And the therapists and even other patients like him who were helping me get back on my feet and feel like living again.

Daniel smiled.

"Thanks," he said, *"I knew He was out there somewhere."*

Tony Roberts

Good Boundaries

*The boundary lines have fallen for me in pleasant places;
surely I have a delightful inheritance.* (Psalm 16:6)

One thing I've experienced in the time I've spent at psychiatric hospitals is that there are many rules. Rules about toiletries and other personal affects. Rules about visits and contact with others. Rules about schedules—times to sleep and meet and eat and rest. Since I am one who generally functions best with good, clear boundaries, these rules haven't bothered me so much. I've benefited quite well from them and have come to appreciate their value. There's a part of us all, though, that constantly tries to get around the rules.

Like the man who found a staff person willing to bring him Starbucks coffee (at a steep price, no doubt) to replace the lukewarm dishwater coffee they served us from the cafeteria.

Like the woman who gained permission to use the exercise room as a space to listen to loud hip-hop music on her boom box.

Like the couple who found a way to prop a broom against the laundry room door so they could get around the "no-fraternization-with-the-opposite-sex" rule.

One thing to learn as psychiatric patients (and people as a whole) is that rules are generally good for us. As chaotic as the world is around us, and as distorted as our mind is within us, rules provide order and clarity to prevent us from harm – from others as well as from ourselves. Rules help establish clear, consistent boundaries within which we can live safely and safely let others live. Only when we have good, firm boundaries can we survive (and even thrive) within this crazy, often unpredictable world.

Praise be to God who gives us such boundaries for life. As the Psalmist says, *"It was you who set all the boundaries of the earth..."* (Psalm 74:17a).

Tony Roberts

Good Friday

LORD, I love the house where you live,
the place where your glory dwells. (Psalm 26:8)

My third hospital stay happened during Holy Week. Having served as a parish pastor for almost 20 years, it was disorienting to find myself out of the rush of this busy, celebratory season. It caused me a good deal of aggravation and unsettledness, so I asked for some pastoral care.

A very kind chaplain came to see me. He listened to my struggle, and spoke some encouraging words. He also told me about a Good Friday service to be held in the chapel. I asked for and obtained permission to go, accompanied by a staff person.

The service itself was no-frills and not particularly inspiring. But, the sights and sounds, even smell within the sanctuary helped nourish my spirit and calm my soul. There was something sacred about this space designated for worship. While there were only a couple dozen people there, I clearly sensed the presence of Christ's Spirit who promised to be there "whenever two or three are gathered in my name." It was a wonderful spiritual boost to an otherwise bleak Holy Week.

I'm not one to claim God dwells exclusively (or even more fully) in such "sacred spaces" as churches and chapels. God dwells just as fully within us and around us— beside a lake in the woods, at a family home, even in prison cells and in psychiatric units. Yet there is something special about those sanctuaries we set aside to worship the LORD. I pray we do all we can to maintain them—for our spiritual well-being as well as our psychological sanity.

The Great Therapist

I cry aloud to the LORD;
I lift up my voice to the LORD for mercy.
I pour out before him my complaint;
before him I tell my trouble. (Psalm 142:1-2)

A therapist is a bit like God in that they both listen to complaints. A good therapist, though, recognizes that his/her familiarity with God ends there. A good therapist resists playing God. A good therapist avoids becoming too enmeshed in our problems or trying to heal our condition for us. A good therapist draws on the healing power that flows from God yet sees that the Source of this healing comes from beyond him or herself.

I've had many therapists – some good and some not-so-good – in my almost thirty-year pursuit of good mental health. I've observed that a good therapist shows great patience, listening to cries and supplications, complaints and trouble all day long, day in and day out. A therapist who persistently yawns or watches the clock can give hurting people the impression that their hurts don't matter. A good therapist helps lift the burden of pain a client carries simply by listening attentively. Being an engaged listener is both a gift and a practiced skill that flows through years of discipline.

While I've had measured success with therapists of other faith perspectives in the past, I now see a very gifted Christian counselor. He does a tremendous job of patiently and persistently walking with me through the darkness of doubt and confusion and helps me make difficult decisions, leading me with the light of Christ. I particularly appreciate that he prays with me (and for me), not to manipulate my choices, but that God would guide me to moral clarity.

While I believe God may speak through therapists of various faith perspectives, the best work I've done has been with therapists who understand my faith story and appreciate how my faith in Christ is an essential resource for my healing. The therapists I've had who have viewed my faith as a crutch or even an obstacle have challenged me to examine my beliefs (which is not bad), but have contributed very little to positive therapeutic change.

While some say "change comes from within," I would contend that this is only true when the Holy Spirit works within us to produce change. The Spirit, who is One with God, is more than just a good therapist. The Holy Spirit is the Great Therapist. Not only does the Spirit listen to our complaints, but always responds with love.

Good earthly therapists lead us to the great heavenly therapist. By entering into our faith story and connecting it to the story of the Gospel, we learn together to grow in the grace and knowledge of the Lord so we can lead healthier, holier lives.

Living Promise

My comfort in my suffering is this:
Your promise preserves my life. (Psalm 119:50)

It is so easy when our lives are off balance to lose hope for a better tomorrow. As we look around at present reality, we are tempted to give up and give in to the voices telling us things will always be just as miserable as they are right now.

In college, when I "came clean" and stopped using the illicit drugs that were in essence holding my psychotic symptoms at bay (yet costing me mental stability), I hit what many addicts call a "rock bottom," I was living alone in a downtown apartment, lying on a used mattress on the floor, working a job stuffing millions of plastic bags into cardboard boxes. I had nothing but time on my hands to look within myself and look around and wonder just what I was going to do with my life. I was lost. I felt miserable. And alone.

Then I started reading the Bible. Again, but like it was the first time. The promise of God's Word is that the life we often settle for is so much less than the abundant life we are promised in Christ. New life is experienced in the person of Jesus Christ, in his healing touch and saving hand. In a world filled with broken promises, this is a promise we can rely on – now and forever.

New life in the resurrection of Christ is more than just a pie-in-the-sky hope for a future resting place for our disembodied souls called "heaven." The new life we gain in Christ impacts how we live each day, each moment. Our lives, even as we go through ups and downs, become more abundant, richer, more full of purpose and meaning. Life

79

begins to make delightful sense in the midst of the messy disorder within and around us.

With this hope in hand, I began to make the most of the present and envision a better future. I left the factory and did a summer mission stint in a Christian community in South Georgia called Koinonia (Greek for "fellowship" or "communion"). Time I had spent escaping with drugs I now spent communing with God and others through prayer and worship. Instead of packing plastic, I was planting vegetables. Instead of isolating myself on an assembly line, I built relationships with children in Bible study and older adults over community meals.

The promise for better days ahead in Christ, when properly received, does not cause us to give up and let the world go to pot. Quite the opposite. Knowing that God cares deeply about redemption, restoration, resurrection, and renewal, we can look beyond ourselves and join God at work making the world a better place – for generations to come.

Working at Koinonia did not magically heal me of past hurts or remove present temptations. But while I was there, God set me on a course away from seeking self-comfort to looking to serve others. I've taken many detours along the road, but I'm still moving forward towards that heavenly fellowship, that divine communion, the kingdom of God on earth as it is in heaven.

Intimate with God

"Because he loves me," says the LORD, *"I will rescue him;
I will protect him, for he acknowledges my name."* (Psalm
91:14)

For much of my faith development, I have been a
staunch Calvinist in terms of divine sovereignty. We love
because God first loved us. Love comes from God for no
good reason but that God is love. We can do nothing to earn
God's love in this life or the next.

For a few years, however, I worshipped and studied
among conservative Mennonites. While I could not embrace
some of their theological assumptions, I did find some of
their beliefs to provide a refreshing corrective balance. It is
good to sometimes concentrate on what we do for God
instead of always looking at what God does for us. Our
actions do make an ultimate difference.

I like the term I've heard many Mennonite ministers use
– it is the "synergy" between what God does for us in Christ
and what we do in response that ultimately results in a life-
giving, saving relationship – one that begins now and lasts
through eternity.

To use a medical analogy, in Christ, God offers us an
eternal cure for physical diseases and mental disorders. This
does not mean that all who "find Christ" are healed in this
life. It does mean that in God's time all who are "in Christ"
will receive new bodies, new spirits and new minds that will
be disease-and-disorder-free. Though we don't see this in
our present life, we trust it will happen in the life-to-come.

It is only by God's free grace that Christ's saving love
comes to any of us. This saving love does not mean we can
sit back and get everything we want. It means we now have

a relationship – an intimate relationship – with One who will never leave us nor forsake us, who ultimately heals us. Within this relationship, we have a responsibility to love the One Jesus taught us to call *Abba,* Daddy. Only then will we divinely delight in the midst of the disordered messes we make of our lives.

Night Time Terror, Day Time Destruction

You will not fear the terror of night,
nor the arrow that flies by day,
nor the pestilence that stalks in the darkness,
nor the plague that destroys at midday. (Psalm 91:5-6)

Many folks with bipolar carry around a lot of fear and anxiety. Some of this may be clinical and need treatment with medication. Some of the fear and anxiety may also be situational. We make poor choices as we cycle and we learn to fear the outcomes of our illness.

I have certainly made mistakes that I deeply regret as I have cycled through depression and mania. While God forgives us as we turn to Him in Christ, we still face natural consequences for our behavior. In my behavior, I have deeply hurt people and am at times fearful of how it will affect them and what I will experience as a result of my sin.

Sometime after I separated from my wife, I tried to fill this void by developing an intimate relationship with a woman I had known in college – who had become a single parent of a young daughter. After building up much false hope and expectation, I crashed and ended the relationship. She threatened to contact my wife. Rather than live in fear, I called and confessed my sin to Alice. Faced with the prospect of public humiliation in a college group on Facebook, I confessed my sin through messages to friends. It was not how I would choose to "come clean," but it was the only way I knew how. Finally, after many agonizing false starts, I confessed my sin to my daughters as well.

Now that I have confessed my sin, I still have the rather difficult work of accepting God's forgiveness. I've been speaking with my counselor a good bit lately on the difference between repentance and penance. I firmly believe that ultimate release from sin comes through Christ who desperately longs for us to be freed by forgiveness. Yet, inside, I hold onto my sinful past and impose emotional penance on myself. I am afraid to live in the freedom of forgiveness and thus fail to "make amends" by moving away from sinful regrets.

What do I fear? I don't fear retribution from God. God wants to welcome me home, not cast me in outer darkness. I don't fear the retaliation of those I've hurt. When people strike out angrily at me, I feel an almost perverse sense of familiar satisfaction that I'm only getting what I deserve.

What I most fear is the unfamiliar freedom of being cut loose from comfortable cages of my own making. The sad reality is I would rather hurt myself than be healed by God, through others. I most fear God's ferocious grace.

The Psalmist celebrates the good news that fear will dissipate in time with faith in the LORD. Even fear based in harsh realities will gradually fade as we come to trust more fully on God's daily provision. The more we fear in this life, the more strength we can find in the faith of Christ.

A Breath

Surely the lowborn are but a breath,
the highborn are but a lie.
If weighed on a balance, they are nothing;
together they are only a breath. (Psalm 62:9)

A therapist once told me one of the good things about having bipolar is that no matter how you feel, you won't feel that way forever. Your mood is bound to change. Depression, which seems to last an eternity in the midst of it, ultimately goes away. Mania, which seems to pass by like a bright blur will no doubt come around again when you least expect it.

One feature of my particular bipolar diagnosis is that I have what are called "mixed states." I can be riding a manic high and suddenly be attacked by a wave of depression, prompting me to become irritable, aggressive, even suicidal. Or, I can be in the throes of depression and suddenly have a manic urge to engage in frenetic behavior – with no warning at all.

These experiences have led me to conclude I simply can't trust my feelings. And I can't base my commitments on my current mood. More than this, if I try to pin my hopes or plan my future on the passing status of temporal outcomes beyond my control, I am bound to fail and run the risk of becoming overwhelmed by my emotions.

The Psalmist recognizes that nothing on this earth lasts forever, and this is good news. Ultimately, the only thing we can depend on is the presence of God in our lives. God is stable. We aren't. God is the Breath behind each breath we take. God will breathe life into us even after we take our last breath on this earth.

85

Tony Roberts

I find comfort in the notion that my moods do not determine my ultimate reality. They are just fleeting feelings that come and go depending on a variety of circumstances and chemical reactions. God, however, is the One (and only One) on whom I can ultimately depend to sustain me through this life and welcome me into the next.

Shining Face

Restore us, God Almighty;
make your face shine on us,
that we may be saved. (Psalm 80:7)

One treatment method for depression is light therapy. This can be especially helpful for people who suffer from *Seasonal Affective Disorder* (SAD). It has been found that for some, more light can help transform a dark mood and give the person just the lift needed to function more effectively.

There is another kind of Light therapy referred to in this verse of the Psalmist. God's face shines upon us when we are lost in darkness and saves us from troubled times. The Light of God's love restores us so we can keep moving forward in faith. This Light therapy is better than the conventional kind in that it is always available and never runs out.

The prophet Isaiah pointed to this Light ages ago –

The people walking in darkness
have seen a great light;
on those living in the land of deep darkness
a light has dawned. (Isaiah 9:2)

There is nothing better, nothing more uplifting, than coming out of the darkness of despair and walking in the nourishing Light God offers in Christ. But as with conventional light therapy, we need to be nourished by the Light regularly to receive the most benefits. If we only turn to the Light for a few minutes one day (like praying before a meal) and then we go weeks, months, even years without encountering it, we are not likely to remain spiritually uplifted.

There have been many days in my journey with bipolar when I have felt so depressed that I shut the shades rather than let the light stream in. There is something seductively familiar (though not truly satisfying) about hiding in the darkness where there is less responsibility, less accountability, less of a chance my flaws will be revealed. Yet, ultimately, I need to let God's Light stream into my darkness if I am to be made whole.

Jesus Christ is Light of the world. As the Psalmist says of God –

... even the darkness will not be dark to you;
the night will shine like the day,
for darkness is as light to you. (Psalm 139:12)

There is no darkness in which we can hide from God. Stepping into the light, and letting the Light of Christ shine in our lives, is the best thing we can do for ourselves – now and forever.

Rest for Your Weary Soul

Return to your rest, my soul,
for the LORD has been good to you. (Psalm 116:7)

One of the marks of bipolar disorder is a sense of restlessness. Often, I struggle a great deal with this. I pace. I sit. Then I stand up almost at once. I toss and turn in bed. There seems to be no rest for my weary soul.

But the Psalmist here assures us that we can lay claim to a promised rest. It is our possession as we grow in our relationship with God. The Sabbath-rest God desires for us in this life, a rest that often escapes us, is fully realized at the end of our extended life journeys. We will then look back on all the LORD has done for us, grateful for the temporary rest we enjoyed, blessed by the eternal rest that lies before us.

Rest is such a cherished and crucial component to a quality life. Centuries ago, Henry David Thoreau wrote, "the mass of men lead lives of quiet desperation." The desperation has only gotten worse in time (and it's no longer quiet).

With technological advances, we try to maintain virtual connectedness throughout our days, all the while sacrificing sacred rest which is necessary to promote spiritual well-being and psychological sanity.

A person with bipolar can be particularly sensitive to the tyranny of urgency these days. The restlessness inside of us is often fueled by the restlessness around us. To maintain balance and continue to function in the world, we need to do more than just take medication.

We need to establish "rhythms of rest" in our daily lives—nourished by prayer (not just worrying), reflection on God's word (not just advice from others), and deep meditation (not just re-tweeting an appealing Twitter message).

The Wrath of the LORD

LORD, do not rebuke me in your anger
or discipline me in your wrath.
Your arrows have pierced me,
and your hand has come down on me. (Psalm 38:1-2)

Some people don't want to think of God as angry. They highlight the portions of Scripture where God is loving and kind and delete the parts where God is harsh and vengeful. But both are there. And both are true.

More than this, to grow in an intimate relationship with God we need to experience all aspects of God's character. The closer we get to God, the more we realize there are times God allows us to experience pain – for our greater good. God may even inflict pain on us to warn us of graver consequences ahead.

God's discipline does not feel good, but it may be the only thing preventing us from certain destruction. Like a parent who twists his child's arm, yanking her out of the way of an oncoming car, sometime firm discipline is necessary. Pain that prevents catastrophe is not cruelty but compassion.

There have been many times in my life where I believe I've let God down. This is perhaps my greatest "fear of the LORD—not fear that God will destroy me, but fear that I will let God down. It is during times such as these that I find it difficult to be consoled, like the Psalmist who says –

I am feeble and utterly crushed;
I groan in anguish of heart. (Psalm 38:8)

Thank God we are not left alone during times like these.

91

The LORD, who is Salvation, hurries to help us. The tumult in our hearts is replaced by an abiding sense of peace knowing God does not leave us or forsake us, no matter how much or how often we disappoint God.

Part of our trouble with the wrath of God is the pitiful examples of how human anger is expressed within and around us. When I become angry at myself, I fret and stew instead of becoming motivated to change. When I've become angry at others, I've often responded by making verbal attacks or cutting off relationships. When fueled by a manic or mixed episode, my anger has become particularly virulent, even violent.

God, however, is far more gracious in His anger toward us than we are in our anger toward each other. The anger of God is directed not at who we are, but at the damage we cause ourselves and others. It lasts only as long as we hold onto the sin that destroys ourselves and our relationships. The love of God, which prompts God to be angry at our sin in this world, will ultimately remove sin from our lives in the world to come. The firm hand of God will then grip us with loving tenderness forever.

Divine Restraint

Yet he was merciful;
he forgave their iniquities
and did not destroy them.
Time after time he restrained his anger
and did not stir up his full wrath. (Psalm 78:38)

If God were to give us what we deserved, we would be in a sorry state. Instead, God is merciful and compassionate. In Christ, God forgives our sin "while we were yet sinners"—when we least deserve it.

Lord knows, I've done many things wrong and failed to do many things right such that I deserve the full force of God's wrath. Yet, time and again, I've escaped with a warning, a slight corrective punishment, reduced consequences, even an encouraging word of discipline.

As people with bipolar, if God gave us over to our illness, to the demons within, it would be disastrous. We would surely be destroyed. Instead, God encourages us to look to Christ. The consequences of wrath for our actions and our attitudes are replaced with love from the sacrificial gift of Christ on the cross.

In the cross of Christ, God restrained his anger from us and redirected His wrath by essentially taking it upon Himself, in the form of His Son who bore our sin, who "became sin" for us that we might be saved. In Christ, the penalty for sin has been paid. We are set free for a life of joyful obedience, delighting in the Lord throughout our days.

A Level Path

Teach me your way, LORD;
lead me in a straight path
because of my oppressors. (Psalm 27:11)

Sometimes I wish it were easier to live with a mental illness. I wish it were more like having a broken leg where treatment, though still painful, is clear and the recovery process, though hard work, is comparatively brief. Instead, treatment for bipolar requires a great deal more trial and error and there is, essentially, no full recovery in this life – only improvement, with many peaks and valleys.

Yet as difficult as bipolar can be, there are still simple truths in Scripture that promote healing. God still shows us the Way through the illness if we turn to the LORD and are willing to obey. There can be level paths along the way for us to follow if we persistently turn away from the enemies within and around us and accept God's guidance.

Just this week I took a key step that is called for in the Scriptures. During worship, the pastor called for persons struggling with mental illnesses such as bipolar to come forward for an anointing of oil and prayer. Before I had time to talk myself out of it, I stepped out of my pew and went forward. There I found strength surrounded by men laying their hands on me in concerted prayer. If only in the moment, I felt a greater sense of power and purpose.

I don't know what God intends as the ultimate outcome of this healing prayer, but I do feel better having gone forward and asking for help. It's been a pretty good week so far. And given some of the weeks I've had, that's saying something. Who knows? Maybe I'm heading down a level path for a while and don't even yet know it? That would certainly be nice.

Addendum: I wrote this meditation three years ago. It has taken some time, but I have been walking on "level ground" for almost a year now. I'm not out of the woods yet, but the path lately has been very pleasant. God answers prayers – not always in our time frame or in the way we most desire, but in the way that is best for us.

Tony Roberts

What We Need, When We Need It

By day the LORD directs his love,
at night his song is with me—
a prayer to the God of my life. (Psalm 42:8)

God knows just what we need, right when we need it.

In the daytime, when the bright glare of the sun is beating down and we are tempted to quit working and lounge in the shade, the LORD's loving-kindness brings us strong relief and keeps us focused on the task at hand.

At night, when we may become discouraged with little or no visible signs of God's love, the melody of a prayerful song can remind us that our lives indeed have had and will continue to have meaning and purpose.

God knows just what we need, right when we need it.

During periods of mania, the last thing I need are bright splashes of apocalyptic visions. So instead God sends me calming people who help keep my feet on the ground.

During seasons of depression, I don't need any help being reminded of my sin. I need help becoming motivated to do something about it. So God sends me encouragers.

God knows just what we need, right when we need it. And in God's own time, God gives it to us.

A Manic Creation?

Let the heavens rejoice, let the earth be glad;
let the sea resound, and all that is in it.
Let the fields be jubilant, and everything in them;
let all the trees of the forest sing for joy. (Psalm 96:11-12)

The Bible depicts creation alive with the joy of the LORD. It may even seem like creation is on a manic binge in passages such as this.

But there is a great difference between the joy of the LORD and manic binges.

The joy of the LORD is a deeply abiding sense of well-being that rises up within us and overflows in expressions of praise. Manic binges are surges of energy that come out of nowhere and feed on themselves until they crash into what is most often a depressive pool of nothingness.

The joy of the LORD can be felt without any particular external stimulus. You don't have to win the lottery or give birth to a child or get a promotion to have the joy of the LORD.

The joy of the LORD simply comes when we receive what God offers us with grateful hearts.

We may have songs associated with our manic binges, songs that define particular periods of our lives. But, there is no song quite so jubilant, quite so lasting, as the one that arises from the joy of the LORD. It can make the field exalt, the trees of the forest sing.

Even the angels in heaven join in the choir.

Tony Roberts

Coming Home

God sets the lonely in families,
he leads out the prisoners with singing;
but the rebellious live in a sun-scorched land. (Psalm 68:6)

Your people settled in it,
and from your bounty, God,
you provided for the poor. (Psalm 68:10)

Many people with bipolar disorder are homeless. There is no escaping this fact. For many of these the best home they can find is temporary shelter in a hospital, respite care facility, even a prison. Some lack a home because they are rebellious, refusing to accept treatment. Most, however, find their condition and financial circumstances just so desperate, they have no better options.

Recently I heard a story that one state is considering renovating old psychiatric hospitals. Not long ago, these same hospitals had been emptied to provide more "humane" community-based care. Perhaps the radical step of shutting off sustained in-patient care without having sufficient alternatives in place is finally being recognized as a failed experiment.

As I reflect on this, I have mixed feelings. I feel some measure of "survivor's guilt," as one who has only briefly faced what it is like to be homeless. Mostly, I feel tremendous gratitude. Here I am with loving family members who watch over my care, abundant food to eat, warm shelter, the joys of living as comfortable a life as a "sane" person. Why? It's certainly not because of my charm and good looks.

I am here, writing this from a comfortable home, on my

98

very own laptop, in the midst of a spacious living room, because of the grace of God. There is no other explanation. All other answers fall short. But for the grace of God, I too could be desolate, in prison, in a parched land. Yet my Good Shepherd has led me to this pleasant dwelling where I can rest in the goodness of the LORD and have my needs met.

Just as it is important for me to recognize God's grace with me now, I acknowledge God's grace with me when I have not known where to turn. When I was nineteen, I shared an apartment with a young man I barely knew. After Christmas break, I returned late one night to find the apartment empty. It was too late to call anyone, and I didn't think I could sleep on the hardwood floor. I had just enough gas to make it to a diner where I used the last dollar I had for coffee.

I spent the night reading my Bible, praying for wisdom and guidance. Instead of these, God sent an overwhelming sense of peace that things would be okay. I had no home on this earth, but I was at home with God.

Even as I write this, however, I am reminded of Woody Guthrie's protest song, "I Ain't Got No Home in This World Anymore." It is sinful to respond to the plight of homelessness with an empty promise of a "heavenly home on high." We need to do all we can to create safe and secure homes for all God's children who are unable to provide homes for themselves. We do this best, however, not through occasional hand-outs that cost us little and keep us steeped in spiritual pride. We do it best through sacrificial love, like Christ. As Jack London once wrote –

"A bone to the dog is not charity. Charity is the bone shared with the dog, when you are just as hungry as the dog."[8]

A Day for Rejoicing

Glory in his holy name;
let the hearts of those who seek the LORD rejoice. (Psalm 105:3)

Rejoicing is not something for the faint of heart. It is not something we should entrust solely to those for whom happiness comes easily. To rejoice in the LORD is to offer up to God our whole selves—body, mind, and strength—grateful for what we've been given and expectant to be put to good use for God's glory.

In Philippians 4:4, the Apostle Paul writes –

"Rejoice in the Lord always;"

Then, because it was so important, he repeats himself:

"I will say it again: Rejoice!"

We can; we *should* rejoice in every situation – through the highs and the lows – because we know God is working everything out for the best, and we want what is best in our lives. When it seems life is not right, when things are not going well, it is natural to feel persecuted by God. We can come to believe we have fallen out of favor with the LORD, that God has abandoned us. Yet, still, we are called to rejoice – not only for God's sake, but for our own. Rejoicing sets our hearts and minds straight – in a right relationship with our gracious God.

I often fall short of the ideal of rejoicing always. When I do, it helps to be around people who have the gift of encouragement. As someone with bipolar, I tend to isolate myself, particularly when I go through depression. At these times, however, perhaps more than ever, I need to be around people who keep me rejoicing along my way.

If you do not have an encouraging friend or family member, I would urge you to find someone in your church to serve in this way. If you do not have a church, keep looking diligently, worshiping weekly, until you find one. It is so much better to rejoice together than to grumble alone. While it may be possible to be "in Christ" and not be a member of a church, it is a little like trying to run a marathon with an amputated leg (and not a good prosthesis).

The best rejoicing comes when we unite our hearts together with other children of God who annoy us, whom we find impossible to understand, whom we love in spite of our differences. As we seek together for the Lord in good times and bad, we lift up a shout of rejoicing that makes our journey more bearable and keeps us moving forward in faith.

The Great Congregation

My foot stands on level ground;
in the great assembly I will bless the LORD. (Psalm 26:12,
NRSV)

Looking back over my nearly twenty years of parish
ministry, I've served some pretty great congregations.
Certainly, there were particular individuals who tried to
make my life miserable (as there always are). On the whole,
however, the churches I've served have been warm and
welcoming bodies of Christ who have helped me function to
my fullest as a minister with a mental illness.

Brothers and sisters in Christ can be a great help or a
tremendous hindrance to someone who has bipolar. I have
been blessed to serve alongside many who have challenged
me to do my best while still loving me at my worst. This
combination has helped keep me relatively balanced;
together we've been able to accomplish some wonderful
things in the spirit of the LORD.

As with the course of my illness, I had many peaks and
valleys in my years of pastoral ministry. It is true that at my
worst, when I needed intensive treatment, church members
had to carry a greater load (though in my denomination,
they often received guidance and support with this). I was
absent for lengthy stretches during treatment. When I was
physically present, I was sometimes so emotionally stymied
that I could perform only basic tasks.

For a good portion of my ministry, however, God graced
me with the ability to balance my commitments, to be
creative and care compassionately as a "wounded healer."
My experience of confinement (a sort of "exile") in
psychiatric hospitals gave me unique insights into the

spiritual needs of persons in prison, home bound, in nursing homes, or hospitals. My struggle to function while depressed encouraged people who experienced dark times themselves. My journey through recovery from addiction inspired many taking their first steps away from destructive drugs and harmful habits.

You might think it improbable that a congregation can be successfully led by a minister with a mental illness, but while it is difficult, it is entirely possible. All it takes is a commitment to be faithful within the covenant God has given us – to keep each other honest and true as we each do our part for the work of the LORD. It can be challenging, but when it happens well, what a testimony it is to God's grace!

Living to Tell About It

I will not die but live,
and will proclaim what the LORD has done.
The LORD has chastened me severely,
but he has not given me over to death. (Psalm 118:17-18)

As a survivor of a suicide attempt, I find myself feeling a strange blend of both shame and gratitude. I regret having attempted it in the first place, but I am grateful I failed. I also feel a sense of obligation to "recount the deeds of the LORD" in rescuing me from certain destruction. God did not give me over to death even when death was my prime pursuit.

The LORD's discipline can seem severe, but it is nothing when compared to our disobedience. God's discipline causes healing pain; our disobedience produces terminal torture. Our self-inflicted punishment leads us to spiritual death while the punishment of the LORD ushers in new life.

In my history with bipolar, there have been self-destructive acts I've committed, many risks I've taken that could have been catastrophic. Driving recklessly is one particular example. I've been in many accidents that could have been much worse, had it not been for God's protection. I like to say (both about my driving and about my life), "I'm a horrible driver, but I know Where to crash."

4. The Basement

God, my soul is thick with dread
And muted tears,
Sinking deeper with every step I tread
And losing feeble years
In silence.

Heavy drags the weight of days
Pulling me under,
And still you swamp me with all of your waves
And deafen with thunder
Yet say nothing.

I look up to your sky to find
There some escape;
Instead the clouds encompass all my mind,
A heavy cloak, a cape
But no flight.

To you I call all day, all night,
My spirit splayed;
The dead cry with me, yet they have no sight
To see your grace displayed
And do not dream.

My eyes veiled from what you have done,
Already close to death,
I follow you into oblivion
With weak and fading breath
And thinning faith.

Darkness is my closest friend;

105

Tony Roberts

Still I pray,
For, with no resolution and no end,
You may yet mend the fray
And bring in day...[9]

~ "Despair" by Matthew Pullar (After George Herbert's "Deniall")

Basements come in diverse forms and serve a variety of functions. I've had everything from a century-old basement crawl space suitable only for hiding from tornados to a finished basement on Long Island that served as a separate living quarters when I was very low.

The basement in my bipolar mind is dark and damp yet soothing almost like a womb. Sometimes I fall into it when I'm least prepared. Other times, I methodically descend one step at a time.

When I was doing my best, while serving in Ovid, New York, I set up an office in our basement. After often spiritually grueling Sundays, I would descend the basement stairs on Monday mornings to pray, become immersed in God's Word, and sit in front of my computer screen, dreaming of new life to emerge.

The basement can be a deep pit we fall into and from which we never come out. Yet, when we have a solid foundation, the basement is the safest place to be protected from the storms around us (and within us). Time and again, God has met me in the basement of my bipolar mind and, after reminding me of His constant care, has shown me the stairs and directed me to face the world with greater confidence, better equipped to serve in the Spirit of Christ.

Crying

I am worn out from my groaning.
All night long I flood my bed with weeping
and drench my couch with tears.
My eyes grow weak with sorrow;
they fail because of all my foes. (Psalm 6:6-7)

I'm not typically one to cry. Apart from a few touching scenes at the ends of movies, and the first times I laid eyes on my children, I'm not sure my cheeks even got wet the first decade of my adult life. So it came as quite a surprise to me when I suddenly started crying uncontrollably in the middle of my sermons.

The first time it happened, I dismissed it as being a strong reaction to a moving illustration; I quickly collected myself, and moved on. The following Sunday, however, the tears came at a much less emotional point. By the third week, I could have been reading the phone book up there and blubbering through it. What was happening to me? Was I going crazy?

In a sense, I was. I needed help. The next day I checked myself into the hospital, and there I would find out that the anti-depressant I was taking not only wasn't working, it was causing me to cycle from dangerous highs to desperate lows. I was experiencing what they called "medication-induced, mood-incongruent symptoms." In other words, I was crying for no good reason, and the drugs were making me do it.

In time, we were able to make necessary medication adjustments. Since then, I have only experienced a handful of occasions where the tears flowed, usually with good cause. Sometimes I almost wish I would cry more, to let out some of the sadness bottled inside me.

One of my frustrations over the years is how, first with my illness and now with my medication, I have lost touch with my true emotions. In the midst of personal crisis, I maintain a "flat affect" and then, much later, a wave of sadness strikes while doing something as basic as vacuuming. It's as if my body has become a test tube and my emotional outbursts are simply expressions of the chemicals poured in from foreign sources, "foes" that weaken me, that wear me out.

It has helped a great deal to have an empathetic counselor. As I share difficult details of my experience in matter-of-fact tones, he sometimes reacts with audible expressions of pain, commenting, "That must be awful," and asking me to reflect more on how I dealt with it. When I see how my story impacts him, I begin to sense what emotional links I'm missing and I feel better, knowing better how I feel.

Being Humbled

Before I was afflicted I went astray,
but now I obey your word. (Psalm 119:67)

It was good for me to be afflicted
so that I might learn your decrees. (Psalm 119:71)

While I've learned to value boundaries, I still struggle with limits. If I am immersed in an interesting writing project, I will work for hours without getting up to stretch or eat or even get a drink of water. Particularly if I'm on a manic swing, I resist going to bed on time. Even while lying in bed, my mind races to all the things I'd like to accomplish.

The week before my first hospitalization, I had barely slept at all. My mind was filled with ministry ideas (all of which seemed brilliant to me). I would formulate the next day's plan while lying in bed, then move on to solve the problems of the congregation one by one, laying out a year, five-year, a ten-year ministry plan. It all came together amazingly, fitting together like an intricate jigsaw puzzle. In my mind, I had solved the problems of the church, my family, even the world. All the while things in reality were falling apart around me.

The crash occurred one cold winter Sunday. I had gone to church around 5 a.m. and noticed one of our signs was bent over. I became convinced someone was plotting to overturn our ministry, but I was determined that we would keep pressing on.

All through the morning I was a ball of energy, flitting from one person to the next. I thought I was saying profound things but now realize I was just creating confusion. In the sermon I was moved to tears over mundane sentences.

The afternoon was a blur of activity. A nursing home service. Home visits. Sermon preparation. I didn't bother going home. And I don't think I ate.

That evening I led youth group. I played the R.E.M. song "It's the End of the World (As We Know It)" while literally bouncing off the walls. A light fixture fell, and I was sure it was a sign the End was near.

Fortunately, I made it home that night and agreed to admit myself to a nearby psychiatric hospital the next day. I had done some outrageous things but had yet to jeopardize my standing as a pastor. God helped me make it to the hospital before I had a complete breakdown.

The experience was certainly a humbling one. While I still sometimes resent limits, I've learned to stay within certain bounds to stay healthier and sane for the sake of the LORD. The "affliction" I experienced being hospitalized and medicated before doing great damage to myself and others has taught me to use greater caution, to maintain balance.

No more bouncing off walls. Now when I listen to R.E.M., I keep my ear buds on and channel my energy into healthy and safe speed walking.

Confined by God

You hem me in behind and before,
and you lay your hand upon me.
Such knowledge is too wonderful for me,
too lofty for me to attain. (Psalm 139:5-6)

Some people (my wife is one) enjoy having the covers securely tucked in at night. I, on the other hand, find it distressing to be so confined. It feels like I'm in a coffin.

Likewise, some people find the thought of God's intimate involvement in their lives to be tremendously reassuring while others find it to be more than a little disturbing (and may reject the notion altogether).

Since I first became aware of God's presence in my life, I've never doubted God's desire or ability to care for creation in even seemingly minute and insignificant ways. Most of the time, this knowledge has given me persistent peace and abiding joy.

For some reason, however, the night of my attempted overdose, I was feeling smothered by the presence of God in my life. Strange as it seems, I wanted a break from being so close to God. My attempted suicide was in part a futile effort to gain some distance, to create some shade where I could hide from the spotlight of God.

Yet, as the Psalmist discovers,

If I say, "Surely the darkness shall cover me,
and the light about me be night,"
even the darkness is not dark to you;
the night is bright as the day,
for darkness is as light with you. (139:11-12, NRSV)

There are still days I prefer to pull the shades and lie in bed rather than walk in the light of God. Ultimately, though, I've come to embrace God's presence in my life as good news. I'm grateful I've passed through the darkness. God's light always shines in our darkness and the darkness cannot overcome it.

Out of the Pit

You, LORD, brought me up from the realm of the dead;
you spared me from going down to the pit. (Psalm 30:3)

When I was first revived from my attempted overdose, I was angry. Really angry.

I was angry at my wife for finding me instead of letting me alone to die.

"Why did you have to find me when you did?"
"Couldn't you just have left me alone?"
"I'd have been better off dead."

I was angry at myself for attempting suicide in the first place.

"What possessed me to do this?"
"What was I thinking?"
"How could I do this to my family?"

I even became angry with God.

"Why does it all have to be so complicated?"
"Why do I have to go through this?"
"Why?"

Fortunately, I passed through this season of rage. It has taken years of prayer, Bible study, and counseling to move through my anger – particularly anger at myself. Yet, I have come to a place of gratitude. I thank God for preserving my life and giving me a fresh start after I had made such a mess of things. I came to celebrate with another Psalmist what God had done,

He lifted me out of the slimy pit,
out of the mud and mire;
he set my feet on a rock
and gave me a firm place to stand. (Psalm 40:2)

113

The saving love of God in Christ now means even more to me than it did before I attempted suicide. God saved me from what was almost certain death at my own hands. Those pills should have killed me, but they didn't. Through monitored medication, persistent prayers, and Biblical guidance, God then set my feet on solid ground so I could move forward in faith, one step at a time.

Salvation is for me now more than a future hope of entering heaven. It is a daily deliverance to live abundantly on earth in spite of my desire to choose death.

The Past is Past

These things I remember
as I pour out my soul:
how I used to go to the house of God
under the protection of the Mighty One[a]
with shouts of joy and praise
among the festive throng. (Psalm 42:4)

After nearly twenty years of weekly worship leadership, I went from being a praise-filled pastor to an exhausted exile. Due in large part to complications caused by my bipolar, I became unable to perform my duties with consistency and went on full-time disability in 2009.

One of the biggest struggles for me particularly in the first months of my "exile" was a nagging sense of nostalgia. Nostalgia may feel good at first, but it can be a deadly demon particularly for someone with bipolar. Ruminating on the past takes me away from present challenges and gives me the desire to find short cuts to get back there.

Longing to experience the way things were in the "good old days," I could try to manufacture a manic episode with something as simple as an overdose of caffeine or sugar or something as serious as skipping my medication. I could pay too much heed to the voices in my head filled with regret such that my sorrow deepens. I could spend so much time remembering the past that my days and nights become little more than re-creations that actually cut into the creative work God has yet planned for my life.

It is good to remember and appreciate the past as long as I don't try to re-create it in the present and wind up with no future at all.

Tony Roberts

Long Dead

The enemy pursues me,
he crushes me to the ground;
he makes me dwell in the darkness
like those long dead.
So my spirit grows faint within me;
my heart within me is dismayed. (Psalm 143:3-4)

Nothing crushes the spirit like a prolonged depression. I've experienced several bouts of deep despair in my journey with bipolar. One occurred shortly after our move to Upstate New York in 2009. I had left my job, going on disability. In many respects, work had been my life, so I was left feeling I had little reason to get up in the morning. Often, I didn't get up. And when I did, I would only make it as far as the couch where I would collapse again and remain for much of the day.

I found this condition appalling. Yet my personal disgust would not awaken my spirit so I could rise from the dead and get back to life. Like the Psalmist, my heart within me was dismayed and nothing seemed to help.

Fortunately, some things fell into place, such as the conception of this book. I got out of bed, off the couch, and rejoined the land of the living. Writing has been and continues to be therapeutic for my mind and spirit. Healing words flow as I look for ways to describe what God is doing in my life in spite of, and even as a result of, the appalling conditions of my life. Dismay that could lead to despair instead turns to hope.

From the Depths of the Earth

Though you have made me see troubles,
many and bitter,
you will restore my life again;
from the depths of the earth
you will again bring me up. (Psalm 71:20)

As I write this reflection, I'm in a particularly dark mood. I look back on my life and see many bitter troubles. I see them in my present circumstances, hounding me with doubts and misgivings. Lately, it seems the only pleasant hours of the day are those I spend sleeping. Fortunately, my dreams have yet to turn to nightmares, yet as I awake from pleasant dreams, I am faced with the reality that I'd much rather go on sleeping.

I can dwell on these troubles or instead focus on the promise of this Psalm – the One in control of our destiny ultimately revives me and gives me hope. Part of the wondrous beauty of the Psalms is the marvelously complex portrait of God they paint. God is much more than a kindly, ineffectual "Papa" to be manipulated for gain. God is also much more than a vengeful Father demanding more from us than we can bear.

God is our deeply compassionate "Abba" who knows we sometimes need to face harsh realities, yet is eager to lift us up should we fall.

When I am in such dark moods that even my prayers won't come to light, it helps to have the Psalms in hand – to be reminded of the light that shines through the darkness. Verses like this give me hope that God is still in control and is working all things out for good, in spite of how the enemy within and around us makes things seem.

117

Tony Roberts

Remembering

Remember, LORD, your great mercy and love,
for they are from of old.
Do not remember the sins of my youth
and my rebellious ways;
according to your love remember me,
for you, LORD, are good. (Psalm 25:6-7)

There are many things in my life I would like to forget.
Things I have done on manic binges. I'd like to have half the money back I've wasted on frivolous spending sprees.

Things I have failed to do in depressive cycles. Like the Christmas when my children were young, and I didn't even get out of bed – all day.

These moments haunt the corners of my mind. They grab me when I am least prepared, and prevent me from moving forward in faith.

When I feel crippled by guilt and shame, I need to be continually reminded to turn to prayer. Through prayer our regrets are transformed by thoughts of God's loving mercy. Our hope is not so much that God has selective memory, but that God willingly chooses to focus first on His love for us and then on forgiving our failings.

Like the Psalmist, as soon as our past sins enter our minds, we can likewise recall the abundant mercy and amazing love of the LORD. We are then set free from our past to best love and serve God in the present and into the future.

From the Depths of Sheol

For great is your steadfast love toward me;
you have delivered my soul from the depths of Sheol. (Psalm
86:13, NRSV)

In the Bible, Sheol is the place where departed souls go
after death to await resurrection. It is sometimes depicted as
a place of torment, but often it is simply a state of tedium
and nothingness.

In my life, I have experienced Sheol as the place I go
when I am in particularly dark moods. I go there for
indeterminate periods of time. I never seem to know how I
got there or how to get out.

Sheol is a dark bedroom with the curtains closed.
Children playing outside, unwatched.
Disembodied voices on the radio sharing unending bad
news.
A lifeless womb,
A tomb of unknown
Lost opportunities.

While in Sheol, it seems I'll never get out, but I always
do. God has consistently delivered my soul from the depths.
With the saving faith of Jesus Christ, I trust this pattern will
continue, and one day I'll leave Sheol behind for good.

For now, I will put my faith in the grace of God through
Jesus Christ, who has descended to the depths to pick me
up. There is no depth to which Christ will not descend to
rescue us. Even the depths of Sheol—in this life and
beyond.

119

Tony Roberts

Afflicted

I am severely afflicted;
give me life, O LORD, according to your word. (Psalm
119:107, NRSV)

Having bipolar disorder may not seem like a severe
affliction to some. In fact, some people make light of the
illness – believing it is "all in our heads," something we
could overcome with more will power or greater faith.

But those of us with the illness do experience it as an
affliction. Someone once said bipolar is a most severe form
of affliction because with it we often lose the very will to
live.

In depressive lows, when the darkness overcomes us, it
seems no light of life can shine through.

In manic highs, when we become so enamored by the
blinding lights of sensory stimulation, those things which
maintain true, balanced life have little room to reach us.

Our hope in the midst of our affliction is found in God's
Word, both in the promises contained in the Scriptures and
the Word-made-flesh in Jesus Christ. Though we are
afflicted, the Word contains life for us – now and always.

While I have found some helpful words written by
others, nothing has shined a light in my darkness quite like
the Word of Christ revealed in the Bible. God's Word not
only shares truths about life, it gives us life to face the truth
– about ourselves, about the world, and about God.

120

Delight in Misery

If your law had not been my delight,
I would have perished in my affliction. (Psalm 119:92)

Oh how I love your law!
I meditate on it all day long. (Psalm 119:97)

They say misery loves company. While this may be true from a fleshly point of view, from a spiritual perspective, misery craves no company so much as delight.

When I wallow in misery due to depressive lows or frustrating highs, I can find no adequate satisfaction no matter who I hang out with or what I do. Often I lie in bed and stare at the walls or pace frenetically around the house or yard.

I have had counselors who have recommended that on occasions such as these, I listen to self-help tapes filled with "positive messages." When I have tried this, I find myself getting more agitated. One major problem with the "cult of self-improvement" is it perverts "faith" in such a way that it becomes a means to an end—towards self-fulfillment. The reward of faith is not self-actualization, but communion with God (which is actually self-denial). Our self, our ego, is crushed by genuine faith – we die to the flesh so we can live in the Spirit.

Instead of self-help tapes, I prefer listening to an audio version of the Bible.[10] This helps stimulate my mind and soothe my troubled spirit. Reflecting on God's Word with as much of my mind as I can muster relieves me from my misery. I may not shift immediately to feeling delight-full, but the delight contained in the Scriptures has a way of seeping in and soothing my weary soul.

Tony Roberts

An E.C.T. Morning

I wait for the LORD, my whole being waits,
and in his word I put my hope.
I wait for the Lord
more than watchmen wait for the morning,
more than watchmen wait for the morning. (Psalm 130:5-6)

It's still dark outside. I lie awake staring at the ceiling, wondering how much of my mind I'll have left by the end of the day. In just a short while I will be having my first dosage of Electro-Convulsive Therapy (E.C.T.) or "Shock Treatment." While I'll be administered only a mild dose, the idea of subjecting my brain to a jolt of electrical current of any amount is a bit unnerving.

Lying in bed, my mind wonders.

"Am I forcing God's hand by seeking this still-controversial treatment?" Or,

"Am I submitting to the hands of gifted professionals who might help me recover to better serve the LORD?"

As I lay in the darkness, no clear answer is to be found. I am left to wonder, wait, and watch for what will happen next.

***

I'm still wondering if E.C.T. was right in my particular case. Given the information I had at the time, I have to believe it was worth a shot. My illness and the aggressive medications I was taking were sapping the strength of my brain and the E.C.T. could have put things in working order for some time. While I found no relief from the treatment, others do. Like any medical procedures, there are no guarantees.

I'm still waiting. Still watching. Still hoping.

Hoping to serve God with my whole heart, body, and mind. Or, at least as much of my mind as I have left.

In the Shelter of the Most High

Whoever dwells in the shelter of the Most High
will rest in the shadow of the Almighty.
I will say of the LORD, *"He is my refuge and my fortress,*
my God, in whom I trust." (Psalm 91:1-2)

Some time ago, I enrolled in a ten-day treatment partial hospitalization program—sort of a refresher course on my road to mental health. I didn't learn much new, but it was good to meet some of my fellow pilgrims on the journey.

I met one gentleman who had really fallen on hard times. He was once successfully working in the legal profession but had lost everything. As he went through the program, he was living in a shelter, looking for adequate housing.

I felt a range of emotions hearing him speak. Mostly, I felt gratitude. I was grateful first for shelters and the people who work in them. Things could have been much worse for him. I was also grateful my life hadn't taken a turn here or there, that I hadn't wound up living so close to the edge as he was. I was grateful for the program where he found the support not to give up as he faced such hard times.

Years later, I found myself in a somewhat similar state of desperation. Because of various factors, one Sunday night in 2012, I left my wife and children. I asked a man I had just met at a prayer group to drive me to a hospital 20 miles away. Based on my mental health history, I was sent to the psychiatric unit for evaluation. I was hoping to find temporary shelter until I could gather the resources (and a plan) to obtain more stable housing.

I spent that night in the waiting room of the psychiatric unit, not wanting to be admitted, but finding that no safe shelters were available. A caring social worker calmly reviewed with me my options. She encouraged me to call on local pastors. I remembered a former ministry supervisor who lived in the area. He knew about my illness and had been a great support in the past. I called him. He told me of three churches that might help, gave me the names of contact persons, and indicated I could use him as a reference.

Within a couple hours, I was sitting in a diner across from a local pastor, feasting on a burger and fries. She explained they would book me in a downtown motel for three nights (more if needed) and provide me with food and other necessities. I could do my laundry at the church and a man serving as sort of a pastor-to-pastors would be in touch to see that my physical, relational, and spiritual needs were met.

Within three days, with the help of family, friends, and strangers, I had signed a monthly lease for an attic apartment at a reasonable price in a nice neighborhood within walking distance of a library, grocery stores, and laundry mats. The bus line was only a block away. For just three dollars, I could get a daily pass and go anywhere in the city I needed to go. Most importantly, I had good, safe shelter.

I am thankful for shelter, in all the forms it comes. I'm especially thankful for the shelter of the One who lives and reigns above. In Christ, we are promised not only a temporary home in this life, but an eternal shelter of the Most High.

I now know first-hand how the body of Christ provides shelter and care and I'm eternally grateful.

5. The Prayer Closet

God shakes the footprints of the sea,
The oceans of the clouds;
Darkness trembles, hailstones flee
At his resounding sound.

He carves crevasses into earth
And tree-trunks slowly bleed;
He weaves the seasons to new birth
First with a dying seed.

A spear has pierced through his own soul,
A crown of thorns his brow;
He breaks apart to make the whole
And he shall show me how.

And so he plants thorns in my side
To teach sufficient grace
And rips away the shame of pride
To shine his radiant face.

Deep darkness is his canopy
Yet he is thick with light;
He spreads the vast, dense galaxy
That he might shine more bright.[11]

~ "Power Perfected in Weakness" by Matthew Pullar (After
William Cowper's "Light Shining Out of Darkness")

I have very plain tastes when it comes to rooms for
prayer, preferring stark simplicity to anything that might
distract me from talking to and listening for God.

When I was first diagnosed with bipolar, we were living in a house that had a very narrow space adjacent to the master bedroom that we used primarily for storage. I set up a desk in this room where I placed my Bible and my journal. I spent much time in there attempting to pray. My mind was basically mush, however, and I wound up mostly letting out sighs and groans, in the hope the Spirit would turn these into prayer.

Later, when I was serving as pastor in the Finger Lakes region of New York, I set up a prayer room at church that had a padded kneeling bench as well as a simple cross and candle on a side table. My prayers had been answered. I was back in ministry full-time and enjoying life as a husband and father. In this space I could express my gratitude to the One who had given me so much.

The prayer closet of my bipolar mind is a place where the small flame of a Christ candle shines light on God's Word. The Word becomes here "a lamp for my feet" (to see where I am) and a "light for my path" (to see where I'm going). I keep a journal here to record my praise for all God has done and list my petitions for my heart's desires. This is the place where I lift up sighs, moans, memories, cries and complains and I listen – carefully and prayerfully, confident God always responds in love.

127

Tony Roberts

No Comfort

*When I was in distress, I sought the Lord;
at night I stretched out untiring hands,
and I would not be comforted.* (Psalm 77:2)

It sounds simple to just seek help from the Lord when
trouble arises. The path, however, can be winding and
complex. Even the most sincere seeker (*stretching out
untiring hands*) can come up short (*I would not be
comforted*). It's more than just a matter of the will. We can't
force our souls to be comforted. It takes more than this. We
cannot soothe ourselves by sheer effort and self-talk.

In my darkest moments, there is simply nothing that
comes to me that I can do to get better. I think of my time in
the hospital when I was receiving E.C.T. Actually, there is
very little about this period I can precisely recall due to
memory loss. But I know that I was seeking help from the
Lord and from caregivers skilled at treating my illness. I
was desperately reaching out and nothing helped. I was only
getting worse. The E.C.T. set off a hypo-manic episode we
had to medicate, and this was followed by another serious
depression. My soul refused to be comforted.

Still, like the Psalmist, I would use the present tense for
the verb. I *seek* the Lord in the day of my trouble. My hand
is stretched out without wearying. Okay, maybe a little
wearying.

But still it stretches out. Prayer that is effective is
persistent even (perhaps especially) when it seems pitiful.

I think of all the nights my wife stayed up with our
children when they were sick and suffering. She didn't
alleviate their suffering, but she cared for them. And they
kept calling out for her because they knew she would hear

them and respond in love. In the moment, it no doubt seemed to them she was doing nothing to comfort them, they were so lost in their struggle. But it would have been much worse had they been alone.

This is what God is like. God does not always relieve our suffering, but God does hear us when we call out and responds with comforting love. The question is – will we acknowledge and receive God's comfort, or have things gotten so bad that "our soul refuses to be comforted"?

Tony Roberts

Speechless

You kept my eyes from closing;
I was too troubled to speak. (Psalm 77:4)

At the worst times in my illness, I've been unable to sleep at nights. I've lain awake listening to the radio, looking for something to soothe my mind such that I might drift off to sleep. If you were to ask me what my trouble was, I would not be able to put it into words. Generalized anxiety they call it. It's a vague sense that something is not right and nothing I can do will make it better.

You might wonder just what the Psalmist gains by expressing here what cannot be expressed. What good does it do simply to identify that *"I was too troubled to speak"*?

It's hard to say. Like the experience itself, it's difficult to put into words. But acknowledging there is a problem is the first step toward healing. God hears these unspoken prayers and, in good time, brings relief.

The Apostle Paul was a man with much to say, most of the time, but even he had occasions where he is speechless. In talking about prayer, he writes, *"Likewise the Spirit helps us in our weakness; for we do not know how to pray as we ought, but that very Spirit intercedes with sighs too deep for words."* (Romans 8:26, NRSV)

Sometimes our most profound and intimate prayers cannot be put into words. Instead, we sigh. We groan. And God knows just what we are talking about and gives us what we most need.

In the Shadow

Have mercy on me, my God, have mercy on me,
for in you I take refuge.
I will take refuge in the shadow of your wings
until the disaster has passed. (Psalm 57:1)

Once again, I've found refuge in the LORD. This time a storm of depression hit due to my lengthy disabling condition and inability to return to work. I've been feeling sorry for myself, sensing my life lacks purpose and meaning. I've been struggling to write, opting instead to escape in a movie, episodes of crime thrillers or senseless sitcoms. When I turn them off, I feel overwhelmed as I see the storm within and wonder if it will ever let up.

But then I look around at the divine shelter that continually surrounds me –

My editor sends a caring e-mail after noticing my time off-line, asking if I'm okay.

A bookstore owner shares a success story of battling mental illness and offers me a free book.

A young friend shares his passion for music along the banks of the Ohio.

A family member wrestling with addiction takes a step forward in treatment.

Instead of feeling sorry for myself, I begin again to feel grateful. This time away from the pressure to perform pastoral work has freed me to express faith through my writing, to explore the Word in words, to connect with and encourage others in their spiritual journeys.

The mercy of the LORD is never-ending.

It particularly comes in handy when we face storms in life.

131

The refuge God provides keeps us moving forward from one state of grace to the next.

Meditate and Moan

I think of God, and I moan;
I meditate, and my spirit faints. (Psalm 77:3, NRSV)

At a treatment program, a man once asked me if I had lost my faith through my struggle with bipolar. I told him I hadn't, but that my faith had certainly been tested. I believe faith is something much more than a positive feeling that can pick you up when you are feeling down. Faith can also come in the form of a white-knuckled clenching to something (Someone) you can't see, but you know has to be there.

My faith has come in stages. At times I've been blessed with the certainty of God's loving presence. Other times, God's presence feels like a curse. I've wanted to hide rather than open up and let God in.

These faith stages have shaped my prayer life. At times my prayer life consists of lying in bed and moaning to God to please make things better, give me the energy to get up, the motivation to do something. Other times my prayer comes in bursts of thought that flash before me so fast I can hardly keep track. Ultimately, I aim for a balanced prayer life that is calming and reassuring. Like most things in my life, though, my prayer life suffers from imbalance more than I'd like to admit.

The message in this verse is that we need take heart when all is not well within us. Meditating and moaning can come in the same breath. It does not mean God has left us or we have left God. The same God we are thinking of and looking to can revive our faint spirits and keep us going – at least until the next prayer.

133

I Hate to Complain, But...

I cry aloud to God,
aloud to God, and he will hear me.
In the day of my trouble I seek the Lord;
in the night my hand is stretched out without wearying;
my soul refuses to be comforted.
When I remember God, I moan;
when I meditate, my spirit faints. (Psalm 77:1-3, KJV)

Complaining can be an exercise in futility, or it can be a pathway to spiritual growth. Prayers of complaint are more a rule than an exception in Scripture. David and other Psalmists (as well as the prophets) complained to God about life in the world and their place in it. Moses complained about the ingratitude of the Israelites. Elijah felt so alone as the only true prophet of the LORD, he prayed to God to die. Jeremiah complained that he was unsuited for his calling. Even Jesus complained to God, crying out on the cross, *"My God, my God, why have you forsaken me?"*

Complaints can be therapeutic if we use them in a cathartic way, to let loose our troubles.

Otherwise, complaints can be corrosive, eating away at our spirit when we can least afford it. Complaints left to linger within us not transformed into prayer leave us more beaten down than when we first started experiencing the problem.

As persons with bipolar, we can certainly find much about which to complain. I complain about things I can't do that others can do and readily stay balanced. Drink as much coffee as they want. Travel internationally. Stay up late and wake up early.

Without prayer, these complaints simply swirl around

and create a spiraling mess into which I sink and become trapped. With prayer, complaints are transformed into creative action that brings relief and gives glory to God. Complaints for what is lacking are transformed into praise for what God is doing, has done, and will keep on doing for those who love the LORD.

Tony Roberts

Help!

I lift up my eyes to the hills—
from where will my help come?
My help comes from the LORD,
who made heaven and earth. (Psalm 121:1-2, NRSV)

Many times in the Psalms, a question is asked out of despair. Where is God? Why does sin persist? How long must I endure? Hard questions are raised to which there are no easy answers. The Psalmist who endures such great hardship struggles with the purpose and meaning of such suffering.

And then, out of the blue, the answer comes. Where does help come from? It comes from the LORD, who made all things and to whom all things return. The answer is beautifully simple, but it's not easy. It's not easy to trust that in the midst of our hardship the God who is in control of all things will also be the One to work things out.

Lately, the hardest question I've had to face is why I do not live with my wife and children. It's hard enough when people ask me about my separation, but it's even harder when I face the question alone in prayer. Was I not supposed to marry her? What could I have done differently to make it work? Should I return home and just try harder?

The seemingly easy thing would be to get a divorce and join the over 90% of folks with bipolar whose marriages have ended. But as the child of parents who divorced, I know that this is never an easy solution. As much as I'd like to believe starting over makes sense, there is a reason Jesus calls divorce and remarriage adultery and no amount of worldly counseling to the contrary can convince me this is God's will.

So, I live with the hard questions. There is no help to be found in the hills of this life.

But, in God's own time, I trust that help comes from the Lord. The Lord who made heaven and earth will one day usher in a new heaven and a new earth. There will be reconciliation, (maybe not as soon as I would like or in the way we would prefer) but it will be for the best, and better than I can imagine.

In the meantime, I wait. I pray. I make phone calls. I write letters. I visit. I try to avoid senseless arguments or pointless accusations. I confess my sin, repent, and obey what God tells me to do. Each morning God gives me the grace to begin again. My help comes from the Lord, and this help will one day lead me home.

Tony Roberts

Defenseless

You have rejected us, God, and burst upon us;
you have been angry—now restore us! (Psalm 60:1)

The Psalms contain expressions of anger at God when it seems God has robbed the people of well-being. The Israelites went through many wonderful highs and terrible lows. There were times the LORD was clearly on their side and times it seemed the LORD was far from them. Trying to make sense of this, they often cried out to God and demanded justice that, to them, meant the restoration of good favor within God's covenant love.

At my worse moments, I have certainly felt God had rejected me, but not through any fault of God's. I felt I deserved it. I felt I deserved to be left defenseless for turning my back on God and not doing my best to love God with my whole heart, mind, and being. I thought I deserved the LORD's anger and wrongly believed that I earned His rejection.

Over time, though, I've come around to pleading for mercy that God might restore me to favor. Time and time again, God has. My life hasn't gotten easier, but I have been restored to a measure of balance that allows me to function on a daily basis. And, in the midst of my function, I have experienced glimpses of abundance. My cup has overflowed. Goodness and mercy has followed me.

Recently I saw an article contending that people who carry an image of God as punitive experience more mental illness. Some would argue that my theology fuels my mental disorder. Or, perhaps my theology is the result of my disorder.

Such views fail to take seriously the strength of mental

138

illness. They also create confusion about the healing power of God. All illness is a disorder condition (sin) that ultimately leads to death. If God were kinder and gentler with this condition, we would be hopelessly lost. But God, in the sacrifice of Christ on the cross, performed the divine surgery that painfully yet permanently produced healing.

It's like a woman I know who was asked if her surgeon had a good bedside manner.

"I couldn't care less," she responded, *"I'm not going to bed with him. I'm trusting him with my life."*

Personally, I'm glad God is punitive with the sin that destroys my health, ruins my relationships, and leads to my death. More than this, however, I'm grateful that God in Christ suffered the punishment for my sake, releasing me from my disorder and promoting my well-being – physically, psychologically, and spiritually.

Call me crazy (I'll even show you documentation to prove it), but my belief that God punishes sin that leads to sickness and death does not make me more sick, or more dead. In fact, by receiving God's gift of sacrificial love in Christ, I am ultimately healed from my sickness and saved from death to serve Christ in this life and be united with Him in the next.

I once conceived a story about an "ugly old ogre" who was feared and avoided by all the townsfolk. It was said the ogre was a shape-shifter. Whenever something awful happened in the village, the ogre would get blamed.

There was a young orphan boy in the village. Before they died, his parents left him a beautiful crystal glass he cherished and carried with him everywhere. One tragic day, he dropped the glass and it broke, shattered in hundreds of pieces. Without shedding a tear, he carefully picked up the pieces and put them in a pouch.

For months, the boy walked around the village aimlessly, taking out the broken shards and lifting them to his eyes, looking for a way to restore the glass. His eyes bled and became scarred from looking so closely. The townspeople looked on in silence, not wanting to disturb his grief.

One day the boy was wandering through the village. His eyes had become so scarred, he became lost. Suddenly, he came upon the ugly old ogre.

The ogre looked at the boy cutting his eyes with the shards of broken glass.

"Stop hurting yourself!" screamed the ogre, slapping the boy on the wrist.

The boy was taken aback. Tears formed in his eyes. And through his tears, the ugly, old ogre became the most beautiful crystal of all.

Silent Pondering

When you are disturbed, do not sin;
ponder it on your beds, and be silent. (Psalm 4:4, NRSV)

While I find too much noise disturbing, I often find silence even more disturbing. (Let's face it, I'm one disturbed individual.) My problem with silence is that I rarely find it silent. You see, I hear voices. More specifically, I hear a voice. It sounds like how I imagine Darth Vader sounds (I may be the only living person with bipolar who has yet to see *Stars Wars.*)

When I'm not hearing the voice, I often have what my psychiatrist calls "loud thoughts," which are random disturbances in my thought pattern that is like traveling with about a dozen small children crammed in a tiny space – like the size of my head.

While I now struggle with silence, I am also a person who has often craved quietness to nourish my spiritual life. I used to make regular visits to monasteries for self-directed silent retreats where I spoke to no one (and no one spoke to me) for up to a week.

For some time now, the noises and voices in my head have robbed me of this nourishing quietness. Medication takes some of the sharp edge off this, but it remains troubling to me that I can't even count on the sanctuary of my mind to find a quiet place.

Through it all, however, God has helped me settle my soul, leading me to desired havens at just the right time, whether it be with a counselor who has a peaceful, engaging presence or a family member who says just the right word to soothe my anxiety. Lately, as I pray, I listen to uplifting music, that speaks to me like a familiar friend. As I listen,

141

words and sentences, thoughts and ideas come to mind (from beyond the lyrics) that could be God's way of speaking to me just as it is my way of speaking to God.

One thing I do to tune out the voice and loud thoughts is listen to audio books at night as I lay down for sleep. There is something soothing about hearing a good reader recite classic poetry, tell a good story, or reflect on Biblical truth.

I do find, however, that I miss the nourishment of quiet reflection. I worry that if God were to try to speak to me, I would be busy listening to someone else. So, when I'm doing better I try to wean myself of the audio. As the noise in my mind wears down, I turn off the audio and tune my mind back into my heart for a good dose of meditative quiet.

I enjoy these seasons where God's promised reward comes to me –

In peace I will lie down and sleep,
for you alone, LORD,
make me dwell in safety. (Psalm 4:8)

Cheer Up

Bring joy to your servant, Lord,
for I put my trust in you. (Psalm 86:4)

I can't tell you how many times I've said this simple prayer. Times I've lifted up my downcast soul to God hoping and praying something would happen to pick me up. More often than not, it doesn't happen. At least not right away.

But that's no reason to stop praying. This Psalm verse is targeted toward those of us who struggle with gladness. If gladness naturally resided in our souls, there would be no need to continually lift up such prayers to God. We need not be ashamed or embarrassed when gladness is absent from our lives. We shouldn't see a lack of cheerfulness in our lives as evidence of a lack of faith. The solution is not to be found in doubling our efforts to be cheerful, but in surrendering our wills to the One who makes us glad.

I used to resent (mostly out of envy) people who would walk around with a smile constantly on their faces. I told myself they were either terribly naïve (thinking everybody who knew better was miserable like me) or hopelessly misguided (fooled into actually enjoying life in spite of how awful it truly was). I've since met many people who have struggled profoundly through dark valleys, such as the death of loved ones, yet who each day walk cheerfully in the light of Christ no matter their circumstances. These people have inspired me to cheer up, in spite of myself.

Divine Remembering

I will remember the deeds of the LORD;
yes, I will remember your wonders of old.
I will ponder all your work,
and meditate on your mighty deeds. (Psalm 77:11-12)

While I regret many of my own past deeds when I've been off balance, one kind of remembering always brings me deep satisfaction and that is remembering the works of the LORD.

I remember God miraculously protecting me the time I spun out on ice in interstate traffic, doing several 360s before gently landing in the snow and mud backwards in the median.

I remember God quietly leading me when I had no idea what I would do with my life, speaking gentle (and not so gentle) words through loving friends and family.

I remember God answering my prayer for a companion in life just days after I had changed my mind about ending therapy and relocating to a new city.

I remember these and many other wonderful moments when God has turned my life around.

For someone who has trouble staying balanced, it's great to know Someone who can balance the whole world in divinely loving hands. For someone who often lives in darkness, it's great to know Someone who shines the light. For someone who often gets lost, it's great to know Someone willing to point the Way.

144

Divine Satisfaction

Satisfy us in the morning with your steadfast love,
so that we may rejoice and be glad all our days.
Make us glad as many days as you have afflicted us,
and as many years as we have seen evil. (Psalm 90:14-15,
NRSV)

For many years, verse 14 has been part of my morning prayer. It's a beautiful request of the LORD to start each morning with persistent evidence of divine love; pure satisfaction that motivates us to rejoice and be glad throughout our days.

As we move to verse 15, however, the request becomes bolder. It is almost an accusation. The thought that God has afflicted us for innumerable days and that we have seen evil for years is a radical claim. You can almost hear a commanding tone in the Psalmist's prayer, *"Make us glad..."*

The more I reflect on this, however, the more I think I will add verse 15 to my morning prayers. While I have not experienced the depth of affliction or seen the evil of many other faithful believers, as I pray, I'm praying for (and with) others as well. I pray this Psalm with my brothers and sisters who struggle to be set free from mental illness such as bipolar disorder. Those who are homeless. Those in prison. Those without family and friends watching over them.

Maybe one day in Paradise we will gather and reflect on the gladness the Lord has brought our way and delight in disorder.

6. The Kitchen

My heart set me off on this life
But grace's pulse is all I know;
My feet soon learned to rise and walk
But grace is the path, wherever I go.
And as my mind has grown to think,
My tongue has learned to teach and wound.
My God, Your grace is everything:
How merciful the sound.

My steps have learned soon to be false
But righteousness has followed me;
My heart has blocked up my own breath
But love has flowed, a cleansing sea.
A covenant from birth to death
Has held me in its open palm.
My God, my life flows out in praise;
You hold me in Your arm.[12]

~"Thanksgiving" by Matthew Pullar (inspired by Christina Rossetti's "The Birthday")

In spite of the irregularities of my disordered life, the kitchen has always been one place I could count on (thanks in large part to my wife) where I could regularly come for nourishment – food and fellowship. From a cup of coffee in the morning, a brief noon-time lunch, a leisurely dinner and conversation while cleaning up – the kitchen is a space to share stories, check in on the day, and look forward to better tomorrows.

In the kitchen of my bipolar mind I have stored cherished memories that have shaped who I am, nourishing reminders of God's abundance through brothers and sisters in Christ, and humorous perspectives that try to make sense of my struggles. Here we can sit down with a cup of coffee and a piece of rich Kentucky Derby pie and enjoy the bittersweetness of life.

Tony Roberts

Highways: Lost and Found

Blessed are those whose strength is in you,
who have set their hearts on pilgrimage. (Psalm 84:5)

The story of the Christian faith is the story of a journey,
a pilgrimage where we are lost and searching to find a way
home. Rather than finding our own way, it is God (in Jesus
Christ) who finds us. God leads home all who follow. The
journey home can be long and arduous, but the destination
is well worth the effort.

My journey with bipolar has taken me down many long
highways of life. At times, I have gotten lost trying to find
my way through my days. Battling my moods, I've
struggled to steer clear of the darkness in the ditches as well
as the blinding lights headed toward me.

One time in college a friend of mine and I decided to
visit a girl I had a crush on who was home recovering from
an illness. We set out without an address, without her
parents' names, and without a phone number. All we knew
is that she was somewhere in a country house in the general
vicinity of Shelbyville, Indiana.

Loaded up with the foolish yet hopeful vigor of youth,
fueled by mix tapes of folk and classic-country music, along
with a full tank of gas, we headed north at about four in the
morning, following the head lights leading us to God-
knows-where. Neil Young serenaded us with "Long May
You Run" (a song about his first car and last love) as my
1967 Plymouth Belvedere with the three-speed Indy shifter
navigated the roads like she knew just where we were
headed. Good thing she did, because we had no idea.

After many twists and turns, we arrived in downtown
Shelbyville and found a mom-and-pop diner where we

purchased two cups of coffee and one breakfast special to split between us (not having enough money for two). Over coffee, we developed our game plan.

There was a pay phone with a phone book dangling from a chain. We looked up her last name and found there were about a dozen options. We checked our pockets and had six spare dimes between us. The odds were even. But we were two smart young men with almost three years of college at "The Harvard of the Midwest" under our belts. We decided to use our deductive powers to narrow the choices. Looking at the ethnicity of first names (we knew they were Presbyterian, so they must be Scottish), the address listings (we figured they lived on a rural route) as well as "intangibles" (i.e. wild speculation), we made a list of the top six prospects.

The waitress brought us our breakfast special and we dug in like two men on a mission. When we finished, we looked at the clock on the wall. Not quite 7:00 a.m. We thought to ourselves, "Respectable people probably don't make phone calls before 8:00 a.m." We had little aspiration to be respectable people, but decided to wait an hour nonetheless.

At 8:00 a.m. sharp, I made the first call. A woman's voice answered, *"Hello."*

"Hello. Would this be the home of Laura Jacobs?"*

"This is her. May I ask who is calling?"

I explained who I was. Fortunately, she remembered me from various classes as we had the same major. It took a while to explain to her that I was with a friend in a diner just down the street and ask her if we might drop by for a brief visit. She seemed stuck on the refrain *"You've got to be kidding me."*

Around 9 o'clock we arrived at our destination. We

visited for maybe 20 minutes.

I can't remember, but I think we brought her a coloring book and crayons (thinking flowers might be too "forward").

The pilgrimage was certainly a blessing. I think we encouraged her. My relationship with my friend was strengthened. A memory was made and the story could now be told. It was well worth the investment of fuel for my gas-guzzling Belvedere. And that breakfast special tasted just right.

*Name has been changed to protect her privacy and to preserve my dignity.

Tumult

You silence the roaring of the seas,
the roaring of their waves,
the tumult of the peoples. (Psalm 65:7, NRSV)

In the Spring of 1989, I was hired along with a group of other seminary students to work at the Kentucky Derby. My job was to oversee ticket takers to make sure they weren't bribed into letting someone enter the gates without an official pass. It was quite a day, working on my feet for over 12 hours in the midst of a million other people. I'm happy to say there were no incidents on my watch. During the race, while everyone's eyes were glued to the horses, I was even able to step away from my post and watch the race at the finish line, as the great Sunday Silence pulled away to win.

Having bipolar disorder, one thing I find difficult to do in ministry and life is deal with tumultuous crowds. When there is a lack of structure and my role is unclear, it can be very difficult for me to hang out and interact with others. I want to escape and find a quiet corner where I can hide and just spend time alone. Fortunately, at the Derby, I had a job to do and I could focus. My role was clear (though not necessarily appreciated by those trying to sneak in the gate). With God's help, I was able to manage the crowd and had a memorable yet exhausting day.

God has repeatedly given me steady stillness in the midst of the tumult to carry out my functions. God has quieted the roaring of the seas, the waves, the tumult of the peoples – at least enough for me to get my job done. This has been true over the course of my illness, particularly in my nearly two decades of ministry.

One particular challenge came when I was asked to do a gravesite funeral several for a community member and her four children who died in a house fire. The father, who was the prime suspect, sat in the front row, with police on either side. I stood in the front, under a large tent. There were hundreds of people in attendance. Local and national media had been cordoned off to the opposite side of the road, but some reporters snuck in. Immediately after the service, one came up to me and asked for a copy of the message.

Through all the external chaos – the carnival-like atmosphere – I was able to maintain my peace, thanks to the Spirit of God. I was able to share the hope of Scripture, not knowing how it would be received by the father in the front row, or by others who wondered how such a tragedy could happen.

Just as Jesus calmed the waves of the storm (Matthew 8:22-27), God stills the roaring of the seas we face in this life. We are able to navigate the waters with confidence and hope for smoother sailing ahead. We experience peace, even as the storms rage within and around us.

Abundance

Human beings ate the bread of angels;
he sent them all the food they could eat. (Psalm 78:25)

When I was first hospitalized for an episode of bipolar disorder, I had no idea how I could afford to pay the bills. I had no guarantee of future employment (and ample signs that I wouldn't be able to work). I had next to no savings. I was fortunate to have insurance coverage that provided some measure of relief, but I wasn't sure how far that would stretch.

In time I came to see just how God provides. My church stepped up and gave me a paid leave of absence. My denomination dipped into some relief funds for pastors to cover some of the extraordinary expenses. People provided childcare, sent over meals, and gave in ways too numerous to mention.

I had a counselor once (more into "karma" than "grace") who, when I reflected on God's abundant provisions in my life tried to explain it as a return on my investment of "good will," But this isn't how it works. God gives us what we need – often through the generosity of the God's children not as "payback," but as a loving gift. The best we can do in response is show our gratitude by sharing this love with others.

I realize many, many people with bipolar disorder have faced much more desperate situations than I have. I am only grateful for the abundance God has shown me and my family during difficult times. I pray this generous spirit might flow through my own words and deeds as I respond to others in need.

Tony Roberts

Prisoners in Misery

Some sat in darkness and in gloom,
prisoners in misery and in irons,
for they had rebelled against the words of God,
and spurned the counsel of the Most High. (Psalm 107:10-11, NRSV)

Part of the stigma of mental illness is the lingering impression some still carry that we bring it on ourselves. Psalms such as this one can contribute to this impression. "Prisoners in misery" are prisoners of their own making because "they had rebelled against the words of God." It's hard to escape the conclusion that somebody with depression or bipolar disorder is (at least according to this passage) being punished by God.

But I don't believe this is the Gospel truth. Notice the initial word "some." I take this to mean that not all who sit in darkness and gloom are there out of their own choosing. It is true that we can make things worse for ourselves. If I do not eat right or exercise or get enough sleep, I know I'm headed for trouble. If I rebel against the healthy and holy ways God has given me to live, I will no doubt pay for it. Even though God is merciful, God is also just and respects the integrity of our free will. There are consequences for our behavior.

I have not created my mental illness, but I can certainly aggravate it. God's desire is not to punish us by making our lives miserable, but to guide us into a Way that leads to life – abundant and eternal. When we offer ourselves – body, mind, and soul – over to the care of the Lord and do those things called for in God's Word, we are better able to maintain a healthy, holy balance that promotes positive mental health.

This is good news for us to receive, yet we need to exercise caution not to inflict it as an undesired "prescription" on others. There are many people with mental illnesses who have, for various reasons, either abandoned faith in God or, have felt repelled from it, prompted by negative experiences within the church (or with individual Christians). The Christian church does not exactly have a stellar history of responding with Christ's love toward people with mental illnesses.

It will take time and a commitment to build relationships one-on-one in order to reverse this trend, but I know it is possible. I've seen this welcoming reversal happen in my own life and in the lives of others. In one church I served, there was a new resident in our community who struggled nearly his whole life with schizophrenia. His counselor brought him to me and asked if the people of our church might befriend him, involve him in activities he might enjoy, and encourage him to be socially engaged.

It took a while. Steve* was not only painfully shy, but he often muttered harsh words to himself, verbalizing his thoughts and then feeling guilty when he realized he was doing it. Over time, though, Steve came out of his shell. He became a regular at our daily morning prayer. Some people in church hired him to do odd jobs. He got part-time work delivering newspapers. We discovered he was quite an impassioned speaker when given the chance, and he became a regular Scripture reader in worship. Most importantly, he built friendships that helped him grow in faith and love. The last I heard, he continues to function well and is a vital member of the church.

I'm convinced the best way to break out of the prison of misery caused by mental illness is through building faith relationships. People with bipolar don't need an overabundance of mental health professionals, but they do need plenty of faithful friends.

*not his real name

Happy or Blessed?

Blessed are all who fear the LORD,
who walk in obedience to him.
You will eat the fruit of your labor;
blessings and prosperity will be yours. (Psalm 128:1-2)

I remember as a child refusing to clap my hands for the song, *"If You're Happy and You Know It"* when I didn't feel particularly happy. Later in life, I learned that Biblical happiness is much more than a fleeting sense of pleasure. It is often translated "blessed," and it refers to a much deeper spiritual sense of contentment that persists in spite of outward circumstances of loss or lack.

I have had periods of depression where I've had to force myself to get out of bed. The idea of putting on a happy face and pretending all was fine with me and my world was repulsive. It seemed the height of insincerity. Nothing short of a lie.

Yet as a pastor, it was my job to convey a sense of blessedness, to pass on a blessing whether I felt like it or not. As a parent, it is my job to show my children the joy of the LORD. I haven't often done these things well, but I thank God for the strength and energy I have received to get it right at least as often as I have.

I may not always feel happy in the "smiley-face" sense of the word—but I am truly blessed. In my relationship with God. In my relationships within my family. In my relationships with all who love me no matter how dark my mood happens to be at the time. Like it or not, I've been blessed—to be a blessing to others.

Tony Roberts

Ten Reasons to Leave Your Psychiatrist

Give us aid against the enemy,
for human help is worthless. (Psalm 108:12)

I have Christian friends who advise me to steer clear of psychiatrists who do not share my faith perspective. I believe God, however, can use even atheists to promote healing should God choose to do so. I've had some excellent psychiatrists and some real stinkers. During one period where it seemed I was getting one bad psychiatrist after another, I decided (in frustration) to laugh instead of cry. I composed a satirical list of ten ways to tell it might be time to leave your psychiatrist.

It's time to leave your psychiatrist when s/he says:

Enough about your mother, let's talk about mine.

Sure, the blue meds are working, but the pink pills are so much cuter.

In my professional opinion, you're crazier than a loon.

Suicide, smooicide.

If you want a taste of E.C.T., just stick your tongue to this car battery.

What was that you said? I was too busy picturing you in the nude.

Before we treat your O.C.D., I'd like you to clean out my garage.

You think you've got problems! My Porsche has a flat tire.

I can see now why your wife wants to leave you.

You think you're fat because you are fat.

This kind of human help is worthless. Fortunately, God provides professionals who care much more than this. It's our job to keep looking until we find them.

Ten Things to Look for in a Psychiatrist

*It is better to take refuge in the LORD
than to put confidence in mortals.* (118:8, NRSV)

Now that I've had fun poking at psychiatrists, I thought it best to look at the positive side. Mostly, I've benefited from quality psychiatric care. I realize many are not so fortunate. Maybe you know someone who is looking for a psychiatrist who can meet his/her needs. First, I should say for most people with bipolar it is functionally necessary to have two mental health care givers: a psychiatrist to prescribe medication and a counselor to provide talk therapy. Ideally, they work together as a team.

While psychiatrists typically do not provide much more than medication management, it is helpful to find one who at least coordinates quality care to address psychological needs from a more holistic perspective. Here are ten characteristics I have found in the best psychiatrists:

Someone who listens to what you say and hears what you don't say.

Someone who provides good treatment options in plain language.

Someone who is reasonably accessible in-between appointments.

Someone who keeps up on the latest meds and yet...

Someone who is not overly anxious to prescribe them all.

Someone who talks with your key loved ones respectfully.

Someone who can smile when you joke about your illness, yet...

Someone who doesn't laugh with you when you are being manic.

Someone with a calm demeanor who can readily ease anxiety.

Someone who respects your faith as a primary healing resource.

I believe we take refuge in the LORD when we seek out trusted servants of the LORD who are gifted at promoting healing. My hope and prayer is that more people will find quality mental health care to address their physical and emotional needs.

How Long?

*How long must I wrestle with my thoughts
and day after day have sorrow in my heart?
How long will my enemy triumph over me?* (Psalm 13:2)

When I was first diagnosed with bipolar, I was told it would be a life-long condition, sort of like emotional diabetes. Along the way, I have experienced some periods of "maintenance remission" where I am mostly symptom-free as long as I remain in treatment. I've enjoyed these reprieves immensely, though I can never tell when they will happen or how long they will last.

Likewise, I can never be sure how long an episode of mania or depression will last. It could be less than a day or weeks on end. Being a "rapid cycler" {*Yipee!*}, I can move from mania to depression in about the time it took you to read this {*Ugh!*} sentence. I once heard of a postcard message that perfectly sums up the experience of rapid cycling: "*Having a Great Time. Wish I Were Dead.*"

With bipolar, I can never know how long a cycle will last. The best thing to do as I wait to cycle is to pray (to cry out with the Psalmist if need be) "How long?" In God's own good time, relief is bound to come.

As I wait and pray, I have drawn on particular resources that have provided me a measure of relief. When I've been at my worst, I've called mental health hot-lines, prayer ministries, and phone counselors. I have a network of friends I have called. Lately, I've been able to express my struggle through blogging and through that now have a faithful prayer partner in Australia. On a few occasions, as I've reached out to others, it has become clear I've needed more intensive help, and I've gone to emergency rooms for care.

Having bipolar is like being on a very scary ride that seems to never end. You sometimes need to sit by someone who will reassure you of safety and remind you the ride doesn't last forever.

Consolation Surprise

When anxiety was great within me,
your consolation brought me joy. (Psalm 94:19)

I was sitting in the psychiatric unit feeling sorry for myself. Looking around at people who had visitors, I wanted to call somebody but felt the phone would only remind me of the distance between us. It seemed everyone on staff was having a hectic day and all the patients were preoccupied. So I sat there, staring at the television screen wishing I were anywhere else but where I was.

Then an aide came up and told me she had a package for me. It was a basket filled with monster-sized fruits as well as gourmet candies and cookies. I looked at the card. The basket came from a reader of my blog who had heard I was in the hospital and wanted to reach out. With some extensive research and no doubt a fair amount of time and money this kind lawyer from Houston, Texas consoled my aching heart. I'll never forget him for that.

Tony Roberts

Revive Us Again

Will you not revive us again,
that your people may rejoice in you? (Psalm 85:6)

For over a year after I went on disability, I battled crippling depression. There were many days in which I felt doomed to live in darkness for the rest of my life. Hope is a precious commodity, and it was in short supply during those dark days.

Then I read this verse (Psalm 85:6). To be revived again. What a hope that offers! And it is a hope based in reality. I thought of the ways God had revived me in the past.

When my Grandmother Roberts died, and I felt lost and alone, I found purpose in playing sports and writing stories.

After college, when I was grieving the loss of friendships and searching for direction, God called me to seminary where I formed valued relationships and gained renewed vision.

In my last year of seminary, when I was struggling to decide whether to leave for an internship or finish out the year, I worried about entering ministry alone and longed for a life- partner. Through prayer and Scriptural guidance, I decided to stay and within a week met Alice, who became my wife.

After seminary, when I was struggling through a chaplaincy internship and feeling uncertain of my call, God blessed us with expectant hope in the conception of our first child, and

I was motivated to seek and receive a call to a local church.

Time and again, I have been lifted up from dark periods, set down on level paths. For God to revive me again, I reminded myself, would be entirely consistent with the divine character I've grown to know and love. This hope is based not on wishful thinking, but lived experience.

Even now, writing this many miles separated from my wife and children, I give thanks to God for reviving me through writing. As I reflect on God's ways and put into words my experience as a child of God, I become more connected – both to other people who read my work, and (more importantly) to God, who revives me through the Word that is eternally encouraging and inspiring.

Tony Roberts

Preparing the Table

You prepare a table before me
in the presence of my enemies... (Psalm 23:5a)

Throughout the course of my illness, I've been fortunate to have a steady stream of income, a way to "bring home the bacon." More than this, I've been blessed with a devoted wife who fries it up for me. I'm not ashamed to admit that we found the traditional gender roles to work well in our relationship. In no way has this diminished my respect for her. I know full well how poorly I would function without her. Now that we are separated, I am blessed to live with my sister and step-mother, who see that we are well fed.

Too many persons with mental illnesses find themselves in positions where they don't know where their next meal is coming from. Even those with material resources struggle with chaos in their lives that works against their need for constant structure. No doubt this contributes to the number of people with mental illness who are malnourished.

One thing faith communities can provide to serve those with mental illnesses is a good meal. And not just for the poor. A church I once served offered a free Christmas dinner to the community and found that more volunteers showed up than customers. These were mostly older and single adults looking for a way to battle depression that often strikes on this holiday typically devoted to families.

When we receive a meal prepared by people who care about us, the enemies of depression and other forms of mental distress can be held at bay by a strong sense of fellowship. Together, we can gather around God's table of grace where we "taste and see that the Lord is good."

166

7. The Study

The road is longer than I thought.
Yes: longer, and much harder too.
The pain is great. Why weren't we told?
You didn't hear Him when He warned you.

The victory songs we sang were lies.
Not lies, but only half the truth.
There is no sign yet in the skies.
Not yet, but His scars are our proof.

What can we hope for, as we wait?
For grace sufficient for our thorns.
And will this see us through His gate?
Of that you can be sure.

And then will day consume our night?
The endless day will start.
And will our faith then be made sight?
Yes, sight to fill your heart. [13]

~ "The Road" by Matthew Pullar (After Christina Rossetti's "Uphill")

My study has been a place of discovery. From a tiny space no bigger than a closet at my first church to a comfortable room with an easy chair, desk, and its own bathroom in Pennsylvania; from our unfinished basement in the Finger Lakes to an austere counseling office where I sat behind a large desk in a high-back leather chair – the precise space hasn't mattered much. What matters are the things I've found out about God, myself, and the world as I've read books, listened to music, and reflected on popular culture to prepare for weekly sermons, monthly newsletter articles, and daily e-devotions.

In the study of my bipolar mind, I have collected books, movies, and songs that have impacted my understanding of my mental illness. The reflections that follow are roughly arranged chronologically, according to when I encountered the works (or when they most affected me).

These reflections are followed by a sermon called "Spiritual Depression" which I delivered on August 17, 2008 at Greenlawn Presbyterian church. This was in the period between when I attempted suicide and when I finally went on disability. It represents, in many ways, the end of my pastoral career, and, ultimately, the beginning of my writing career.

Time and space do not permit me to share all the resources that have influenced my life with bipolar, so I've included a section at the end of "The Study" called "On the Shelf" that points to some practical places you might go for further information and support.

From One Unquiet Mind to Another

When I was first diagnosed with bipolar, the portrait painted for me of my future was bleak. I was told that I would never work again as a pastor, that I would likely get divorced, and that I would spend the rest of my life in and out of mental hospitals. After sharing the bad news, the staff tried to encourage me by handing me a crayon and telling me I could draw whatever I liked.

Fortunately, my psychiatrist was more hopeful. He encouraged me to read a book that had just come out called *An Unquiet Mind* by Kay Redfield Jamison. Jamison is considered by many to be the world's leading expert on bipolar disorder. She also has the illness.

Unquiet Mind details her rise and fall and rise again. It's not a how-to book, but a simple and profound testimony that bipolar is not a death sentence or a diagnosis that necessarily leads directly to disability. The book is vivid in its depictions of reality from a manic-depressive (the term Jamison prefers) point of view. One (somewhat lengthy) quote captures this well:

There is a particular kind of pain, elation, loneliness, and terror involved in this kind of madness. When you're high it's tremendous. The ideas and feelings are fast and frequent like shooting stars, and you follow them until you find better and brighter ones. Shyness goes, the right words and gestures are suddenly there, the power to captivate others a felt certainty. There are interests found in uninteresting people. Sensuality is pervasive and the desire to seduce and be seduced irresistible. Feelings of ease, intensity, power, well-being, financial omnipotence, and euphoria pervade one's marrow. But, somewhere, this changes. The fast ideas are far too fast, and there are far too many; overwhelming confusion replaces clarity. Memory goes. Humor and absorption on friends' faces are replaced by fear and concern. Everything previously moving with the grain is now against-- you are irritable, angry, frightened, uncontrollable, and enmeshed totally in the blackest caves of the mind. You never knew those caves were there. It will never end, for madness carves its own reality.[14]

After reading Jamison's inspiring story, I saw no reason why I couldn't return to work and family life and enjoy my best years in spite of my diagnosis. For over a decade, I was able to do just this.

Jamison's gift for encouragement has touched the lives of so many people struggling with bipolar. She has also likely contributed to the existence of future generations. She served as a consultant on the Human Genome project, advocating for the value of life even with bipolar. It is not just a genetic mutation that needs to be "therapeutically removed" from the human population. People with bipolar have served the world through artistic expression, scientific exploration, governmental leadership, and educational advancement.

As Jamison reflects on the question of whether bipolar has contributed anything positive to her life, she writes this:

I honestly believe that as a result of it I have felt more things, more deeply had more experiences, more intensely; loved more and been more loved; laughed more often for having cried more often; appreciated more the springs for all the winters; worn death "as close as dungarees," appreciated it — and life, more; seen the finest and most terrible in people, and slowly learned the values of caring, loyalty, and seeing things through... [15]

Sometimes I find it difficult to separate myself from my illness. But I agree with Jamison that our unquiet minds stir us to discover more about the world and express it with greater clarity than if we were somehow cured.

Tony Roberts

The Dream Team is a Nightmare

My memory is fuzzy around the period after my initial diagnosis in 1995. I'm not sure if I saw the movie *The Dream Team* then or if I had seen it earlier. I do remember that when I first saw it, I thought it was hilarious. Composed of a cast with Christopher Lloyd, Peter Boyle, and Michael Keaton as psychiatric patients running rampant in New York City, what's not to love?

After viewing it in 2013, I was left to wonder, "What drugs was I taking to have enjoyed it so much?" My answer is, "Probably not enough."

I won't spoil the movie any more than it does itself. I will simply detail my three major problems with the film.

First, the underlying message is that if people with psychosis just stop taking their medication and face extremely stressful challenges, they naturally come to their senses and are healed. I realize in 1989, there were still a lot of psychiatric patients overprescribed massive amounts of Thorazine, but a new generation of psycho-tropics was emerging and, in many states, long-term institutional care was no longer an option. The film takes place outside New York City, and I'm pretty sure New York was either closing or had closed its state psychiatric hospitals by then. The movie tries to be *One Flew Over the Cuckoo's Nest* and fails miserably.

Second, the movie laughs *at* (rather than *with*) psychotics. The characters are one-dimensional and, apart from one family scene (with Christopher Lloyd's character and his daughter) that is supposed to be touching, it simply mocks characteristics of stereotypical psychotics rather than reveals humorous foibles they find in life.

Third, it's just not that funny. The funny bits could

easily fit in a trailer. In fact, I can only remember one –
when Peter Boyle's character (who thinks he's Jesus Christ)
tells a man on a gurney to "Rise and walk." The man gets
up and falls. Okay, now that I think of it, that isn't even
funny.

Perhaps the movie was a propaganda film for states
closing psychiatric hospitals in the vain hope that
community-based care would be more humane. If this is the
case, I suppose it succeeds on a certain perverse level. Who
wouldn't want to live next door to the Savior of
humankind? Especially when he is off his meds.

Tony Roberts

Song for Vincent Reconsidered

I was in high school when I first heard Don McLean's tribute song to Vincent Van Gogh (also known as "Starry, Starry Night"). I found the song captivating and beautiful. One line of the song, however, troubled me. Near the end, as McLean reflects on the tragic death of the great artist, he sings,

"This world was never meant for one as beautiful as you."

This line infuriated me. I saw it as a glorification of suicide. I thought of my Grandpa Joe Etsy and how angry I was at him for leaving his family behind. Beautiful? I don't think so.

When I reflected on this on my blog in early 2013, I received a very passionate and thoughtful reply that completely changed my interpretation of this line, and enhanced my appreciation for the song.

From: Julia
Re: the line in McLean's song

"This world was never meant for one as beautiful as you," I did not think he was suggesting suicide as the only resolution; in fact, quite the opposite. Note the entire context: "when no hope was left inside...you took your life as lovers often do. BUT (emphasis mine) I could have told you, Vincent, this world was never meant..."

To me, the "but I could have told you" implies that his tragic death might have been prevented if Vincent could have come to understand and accept that he would never be

174

fully understood or appreciated by the world. Acceptance of this might have lessened the frustration and sorrow that exacerbated his depression, especially if that understanding came from a sympathetic friend, which McLean wistfully imagines he could have been.

It's easy, of course, for us to imagine in hindsight that we would have been the sympathetic friend Vincent lacked. What haunts me is wondering how many Vincents we all pass by every day, without seeing...

Tony Roberts

Acedia and Me:
A Mental Health Perspective

The first year I was on disability, I found it difficult to get out of bed. Before I conceived of writing this book of meditations, I didn't know what to do with myself. We lived on a seven-and-a-half acre homestead and there was plenty to do, but I seem to be pathologically allergic to real work.

While at the library one day, I picked up a book by poet and spiritual essayist Kathleen Norris called *Acedia and Me: A Marriage, Monks, and a Writer's Life*. Norris is a wonderful writer, and there is much to be said for the book, but my purpose here is to briefly unpack what she reveals about the elusive yet pervasive condition known as "acedia."

Exploring early monastic literature, Norris discovers that before there were seven deadly sins, there were actually eight vices, one of which is the difficult-to-define acedia. Norris describes it this way:

"The demon of acedia—also called the noonday demon—is the one that causes the most serious trouble of all. . . He makes it seem that the sun barely moves, if at all, and . . . he instills in the heart of the monk a hatred for the place, a hatred for his very life itself."[16]

Norris is careful to distinguish spiritual acedia from clinical depression. She is not suggesting psychological disorders are the result of demonic spirit.

"The boundaries between depression and acedia are notoriously fluid; at the risk of oversimplifying, I would

176

suggest that while depression is an illness treatable by counseling and medication, acedia is a vice that is best countered by spiritual practice and the discipline of prayer."[17]

Not everyone who battles acedia has a psychological disorder. But, many with psychological disorders must battle acedia. To engage in this spiritual warfare, we need the full armor of God—Bible study, daily prayer, weekly worship, and faithful fellowship.

Like *An Unquiet Mind*, *Acedia and Me* is the story of one woman's encounter with spiritual dis-ease. It is more descriptive than prescriptive, but as the demon is detailed, we become better aware of who our enemy is so we can better prepare to win the war.

Tony Roberts

A Companion in Darkness

After completing the first draft of my spiritual memoir, I sent it to several friends who had shown an interest in my reflections. One friend wrote back and asked if I had read the book *Darkness Is My Only Companion: A Christian Response to Mental Illness* by Kathryn Greene-McCreight. I had not, but I soon picked up a copy at my local library.

Greene-McCreight is an Episcopal priest who, like me, battles bipolar. *Darkness Is My Only Companion* is her attempt to wrestle with her illness and make sense of it in light of the church's teachings. It is an honest, searching work that serves well to provoke thought about how Christians can best respond to the needs of those with bipolar.

One strength of Greene-McCreight's approach is that she provides a balanced, Biblical perspective on healing. Quoting Ecclesiastes 4:12, she writes,

"'A three-fold cord is not quickly broken.' The three cords to my rope were the religious (worship and prayer), the psychological (psychotherapy), and the medical (medication, electroconvulsive therapy, and hospitalization)."[18]

In addition to being a parish priest, Kathryn is a wife and mother whose bipolar symptoms first appeared when her children were quite young. She agonizes over the dilemma of her depression:

I would avoid the family, in part because the noise was so painful to me that I could not stand it and in part because I did not want to make others miserable by my presence. I did

178

not understand at that time that my family and friends truly missed me. I later came to realize this and moved my nest from our bed to the living room as I improved. I was silent and still unable to move, but at least I was there, with the children and my husband.[19]

One of the greatest blessings of this book for me was found in Greene-McCreight's thoughtful theological and pastoral reflections on the Christian response to suicide. She writes,

"... a Christian's suicide, especially that of a Christian teacher or pastor, is the final act of disobedience, of betrayal of the Creator. Of course, I know this is often not consciously chosen, or when it is conscious, it is a choice born of tremendous unbearable pain."[20]

She goes on to consider those left behind, citing an example of a friend's pastor who suffocated himself. Finally, she acknowledges,

"... the stakes are high: the Christian's suicide in effect contradicts every good word about God one could ever have preached, undoes every good work dedicated to God and neighbor that one could ever have accomplished. I cannot allow myself so to undermine my very life's work. I pray to God for strength to hold on."[21]

The Hollywood Silver Linings Playbook:
Fake Right, Go Wrong

To do justice to *Silver Linings Playbook*, I'm dividing this meditation in three parts. First, I will tell you how great a movie it is and encourage you to see it. Then, I will tell you how wrong the movie's message is in the end. I will give the final word, though, to one of my blog readers who experienced the ending quite differently.

First, the movie is great. Never has a film been made that so accurately and compassionately depicts the turmoil of people who battle bipolar. As Pat (Bradley Cooper) plows through volumes of literature (reacting to *A Farewell to Arms* by throwing it out the window), erupts in a rage over his wedding song played at his psychiatrist's office, and explodes in violence toward his mother when he can't find his wedding video, we see the ravages of the illness. Yet, the loving person of Pat is not far away, as he moves quickly to remorse and regret.

Cooper's portrayal of Pat is nothing short of brilliant. Standing on-screen beside Robert DeNiro (as Pat, Sr.), Cooper more than holds his own. Jennifer Lawrence does a competent job as the fragile, volatile, strong-willed Tiffany. The supporting cast contributes greatly, particularly Chris Tucker, as the comical delusional psychotic creatively looking for a way out of the hospital.

Not only does the movie accurately portray one man's mental illness, but also the "craziness" in the family system within which so many bipolar folks live and breathe and have their being. From Pat Sr.'s gambling addiction, to the barely controlled marital rage of Pat's friend Ronnie (John Ortiz). Even beyond the family system, the scenes where a neighborhood kid drops in wanting to take a reality video for a class on mental illness is spot-on. The craziness of bipolar is not an isolated aberration. It is embedded in our culture.

Finally, the story itself (until the end) is exquisitely complex. I often find myself trying to anticipate resolution as I watch films, and this one had my mind going in multiple directions at the same time. It was like a very enjoyable roller-coaster ride.

But then, there is the end. Every move has a message that is driven home by the way the movie ends. While the primary intended message of this movie may well have been to de-stigmatize mental illness (in which case, it succeeded), there was a more subversive message that won the day in the end, likely as a result of Hollywood's formulaic equation for romantic comedies.

The *Hollywood Silver Linings Playbook* for battling bipolar has basically seven steps:

• Meet a woman with a mental illness who has stopped taking her meds, is lost in grief and is actively pursuing a sexual addiction.

• When you are taken aback by her sexual aggressiveness (an offer *"to f@#$ me, as long as the lights are on"*), start back on your meds to mellow out.

• Let down your physical and psychological boundaries when she pretends to be your wife.

• When you discover she has lied and deceived you, go through with your commitment to her.

• When she tragically tries to pick up another man at a bar, rescue her.

• Leave your wife and profess your undying love for this very ill woman.

• Snuggle together on a comfy chair trapped in a system that perpetuates the chaos within you.

When I shared this reflection on the movie in a blog post, I received a wonderful response, including many comments from viewers who reacted quite differently than me to the movie. To balance this meditation and motivate you to see the film, I'd like to close with a comment left by one reader:

You make some good points here…. but I think part of Mr. Cooper's character's problem was unrealistic hope for a marriage that had run its course. For sure not every bi-polar patient should jump ship and look for a replacement. But love is indeed healing. Yes, Hollywood loves romance. But I believe the romance in this one.

Ricocheting Madly In-Between:
The Emotional Life of Sylvia Plath

At age 19, Sylvia Plath was a top scholarship student at a prestigious college, a published (for pay) author, and a vibrant, blond beauty with many suitors. Yet, all was not well within her. She writes in her journal, *"I have much to live for, yet unaccountably I am sick and sad."* [22] Rather than talk to someone about it (a friend advised her to see a psychiatrist), she tries some encouraging self-talk, and she is able to temporarily "pick herself up by her bootstraps."

"I have started on the rise upward after bouncing around a little on rock bottom. I know I am capable of getting good marks: I know I am capable of attracting males. All I need to do is keep my judgment, sense of balance and philosophic sense of humor, and I'll be fine, no matter what happens." [23]

Yet, her very next journal entry reveals that the benefits of self-therapy are short-lived. She falls deeper into the pit of despair.

"Now I know what loneliness is, I think. Momentary loneliness, anyway. It comes from a vague core of the self – like a disease of the blood, dispersed throughout the body so that one cannot locate the matrix, the spot of contagion." [24]

Plath, however, does not let this "disease of the blood" incapacitate her. She continues to write, to go to classes, to go out on dates. But inside, she is dying on the vine.

"God, but life is loneliness, despite all the opiates, despite the shrill tinsel gaiety of parties with no purpose, despite the false grinning faces we all wear."[25]

Plath talks very little about her family in her early journals. One entry, however, does reveal her mother's concern for her emotional health – a concern not well received by Sylvia.

"My enemies are those who care about me most. First, my mother. Her pitiful wish that I 'be happy.' Happy! That is indefinable as far as states of being."[26]

While the young Plath perceives happiness as unattainable, she does believe behavioral choices contribute to emotional states.

"I have the choice of being constantly active and happy or introspectively passive and sad. Or I can go mad by ricocheting in between."[27]

At 19, however, Plath saw life as very much worth living.

"For all my despair, for all my ideal, for all that – I love life. But it is hard, and I have so much – so very much to learn."[28]

Tragically, this love of life and desire to learn dissipated over the next decade. At age 30, Sylvia Plath, on the verge of publishing her now-classic novel *The Bell Jar*, committed suicide.

Spiritual Depression

Some people think only those with weak wills or a lack of faith suffer from depression. The truth is even the most faithful Christians can get depressed. Some experience acute situational depression – such as when a loved one dies or a relationships ends. Others battle chronic clinical depression, due to their particular brain chemistry.

The Bible is filled with examples of believers who battle depression. While it offers us no simple cure, Scripture does provide spiritual principles and practices that can help us move through the dark nights of our souls to the bright morning sun, the light of Christ.

Depression is an illness, a disease that impacts us not just emotionally, but also physically and spiritually. Thanks be to God, medical science now has a number of ways to treat the symptoms of depression – with prescribed medication, talk therapy, monitored nutrition, and regulated exercise. But how do we treat depression spiritually?

Psalm 42 shows a model for moving through the darkness of depression in the light of God's love. First, we recognize our spiritual need. Beginning in verse one and two,

As the deer pants for streams of water,
so my soul pants for you, my God.
My soul thirsts for God, for the living God.

There is no doubt depression has physical and emotional causes, but there is also a strong spiritual component. For healing to happen, we need to recognize our longing for God, to seek God where He may be found. The deer needs water not only to relieve thirst, but in order to survive.

185

Likewise, we need God in our daily lives to save us from self-destruction, from spiritual death.

Doctors, therapists, and other health care providers can contribute to recovery, but they can't produce healing. God alone in Jesus Christ is the Great Physician. For healing to happen, we need to look to the Lord.

Later in verse 2, the Psalmist asks,

When can I go and meet God?

The Psalmist is in exile, a stranger in a stranger land. He is separated from the fellowship of faith, restricted from worshiping God with other believers. This isolation compounds his despair. Later, in verse 4, he brings to mind days gone by.

These things I remember
as I pour out my soul:
how I used to go to the house of God
under the protection of the Mighty One
with shouts of joy and praise
among the festive throng.

These are bittersweet memories for the Psalmist. He is reminded of the joy and thanksgiving he once shared within the faith family. At the same time, he is made aware of what is now missing from his life.

I can greatly appreciate the Psalmist's struggle being separated from his faith family. The time I was away from church during my hospitalization, I felt a huge void in my life. It was a tremendous blessing to hear from so many of you. Your faithful prayers, encouraging notes and cards, phone calls, and meals for my family greatly enhanced my healing process. I was daily reminded of the depth of God's love reaching out through the body of Christ.

The first step toward healing from depression is to recognize our spiritual thirst for God. We can then call on God for help. Often, God's help comes from within the body of Christ – through encouraging words and acts of kindness.

Depression is a powerful disease from which there are no quick fixes. In verse 3, the Psalmist cries out from the depths, *"My tears have been my food day and night..."*

He is overcome by emotions that seem to have little basis in outward circumstances. The weight of his despair is overwhelming.

In my years as a pastor, I've known many people who, as they fought depression, stop coming to church. This is a common strategy the enemy uses—divide and conquer struggling souls by isolating them from the fellowship of faith.

I visited one such woman and, as our visit ended, I encouraged her to come to church on Sunday. She replied,

"I really can't. I'm afraid I would just break down."

I thought about it a bit, then said,

"That would be great if you did. The Bible tells us that the sacrifices pleasing to God are a broken and contrite spirit. God promises us that those who sow in tears will reap with songs of joy."

We could all benefit if we were to break down in tears from time to time. And what better place to do it than in God's sanctuary, the living room of our Heavenly Father.

To compound his troubles, the Psalmist is under enemy attack. In verse 3, he notes that people, "say to me all the day long, 'Where is your God?'" Verse 10 adds to this, describing the effects of these attacks,

My bones suffer mortal agony
as my foes taunt me,
saying to me all day long,
"Where is your God?"

It's sad to say, but many people in the world are eager to kick us when we are down. These enemies of the Psalmist may be calling into question the existence or power of God. More likely, however, they are casting doubt on the Psalmist's faith. It's as if they are saying, *"You say you believe in God, why then are you suffering?"*

Jesus went through similar mocking as he hung on the cross. One of the thieves hanging beside him said, *"If you are the Christ – save yourself and us!"*

Such taunts are bound to aggravate our depression. When facing such attacks, we need to call on the Spirit of Christ who, while hanging on the cross, was able to say to his accusers, *"Father, forgive them, they know not what they do."*

In Psalm 42, the Psalmist tries to make sense of his depression, to be freed from its grip. In verse 5, he asks himself,

Why, my soul, are you downcast?
Why so disturbed within me?

Often with clinical depression, we cannot find an external source or cause that would account for the depth of our sorrow. We may simply wake up one morning and find it is next to impossible to get out of bed. This may persist for weeks, months, even years.

One of the most effective forms of treatment for

depression is called Cognitive-Behavioral Therapy. This approach recognizes that what we think governs how we feel as well as how we behave. If we think life is just a meaningless series of events, we are likely to feel depressed and lack the motivation to do anything about it. If, however, we replace this negative thought with a more positive one, we can overcome feelings of despair and move toward healing.

This is just the sort of thing the Psalmist does at the end of verse 5. He speaks to his own soul, saying,

Put your hope in God,
for I will yet praise him,
my Savior and my God.

The enemy wants us to believe when we feel depressed that nobody cares, that our life lacks meaning and purpose, that God (if there is a God) is too busy with other things or is simply unconcerned about us. God, in Christ, constantly challenges these lies.

In Matthew 10, Jesus says,

Are not two sparrows sold for a penny? Yet not one of them will fall to the ground outside your Father's care. And even the very hairs of your head are all numbered. So don't be afraid; you are worth more than many sparrows. (vv. 29-31)

The God who created us in His image cares deeply about us and wants us to live in His love. The God who, in Jesus Christ, gave His life to set us free from sin and death, shines His light in the darkness of our despair. God's gift to us through faith in Christ is a Spirit of joy. We may sow in tears, but with Christ, we will reap with laughter.

As we pass through dark valleys in our lives, it is good to remind ourselves of the power of God's love. Picking up in verse 6 of Psalm 42, we read,

My soul is downcast within me;
therefore I will remember you
from the land of the Jordan,
the heights of Hermon—from Mount Mizar.
Deep calls to deep
in the roar of your waterfalls;
all your waves and breakers
have swept over me. (vv. 6-7)

The Psalmist is saying in this poetic imagery that God demonstrates His tremendous power in the world, and in our lives. The God who produces waterfalls, waves, and breakers can certainly satisfy our thirsty souls. God is certainly strong enough to lift us up when we are cast down.

Though the Psalmist may not feel as if God is with him in the moment, he does not let this feeling undermine his faith. In verse 8, he proclaims,

By day the LORD directs his love,
at night his song is with me—
a prayer to the God of my life.

We can't let our feelings undermine our faith. In Jesus Christ, God is with us, whether it feels like it or not. By day and by night, we do well to remind ourselves of God's loving presence.

One thing I highly recommend for you as you go through dark valleys is, like the Psalmist, you keep a song in your hearts. There are so many hymns and praise songs that lift us up when we are down. We do well not just to sing these in church, but throughout the week.

Paul writes to the Ephesians, and to us, to speak...

... to one another with psalms, hymns, and songs from the Spirit. Sing and make music from your heart to the Lord, always giving thanks to God the Father for everything, in the name of our Lord Jesus Christ. (Ephesians 5:19-20)

Through music, the Holy Spirit lifts up our hearts and minds so that we can feel the warmth of God's love, and share this love in our relationships – with God and with each other.

The demon of depression can be tenacious, voracious, and debilitating. Even when we draw on the resources of our faith in Christ, the darkness may persist. In Psalm 42:9, the Psalmist returns to his complaint,

I say to God my Rock,
"Why have you forgotten me?
Why must I go about mourning,
oppressed by the enemy?"
My bones suffer mortal agony
as my foes taunt me,
saying to me all day long,
"Where is your God?"

We may believe with all our hearts and mind that God is with us in Christ. And yet, it feels like God is nowhere to be found. The Psalmist reveals how attacks from the enemy can call our faith into question.

When facing depression, often our biggest enemy comes

from within. We struggle with self-doubt, question our value, even wonder if we have faith. Our adversary works hard to infiltrate the minds of believers and plant ideas that discourage us, that keep us growing in our relationship with Christ. To counter this attack, we need to *"set our minds on things above"* – to fill our minds with spiritual thoughts.

Through depression, the enemy attempts to insinuate doubt in our minds that we have a God in Christ who cares deeply about us. Our adversary tries to divide and conquer us, getting us to isolate ourselves from God and from God's people. Satan manipulates our feelings such that we can begin to doubt our relationship with Christ.

The good news is that the only power the enemy has within us is the power of suggestion. We can win the spiritual battle as we open our hearts to the living Lord. Psalm 42 concludes with the refrain in verse 11,

Why, my soul, are you downcast?
Why so disturbed within me?
Put your hope in God,
for I will yet praise him,
my Savior and my God.

When you go through depression, you may have no idea where this feeling is coming from. But you can know that you are never alone. Jesus says, *"I am with you always, even to the end of the age."*

You can also know with the certainty of faith that God will lead you through the darkest valleys with the Light of his love. With faith in Christ, one day, we will rejoice together with all God's children.

There will be no more tears.

No more suffering.

192

No more sorrow.

Only praise to the One who created us in love, in whom there is no darkness – only light. The Light of Christ.

On the Shelf

If someone you know is displaying symptoms such as...

Rapid, repetitive talk
Restlessness
Loss of sleep
Excessive spending
Increased sexual activity
Risk-taking behaviors
Extreme loss of energy
Loss of appetite
Obsessively morbid conversation
Oversleeping
Lack of interest in typically pleasurable activities

... s/he may have bipolar disorder. You can't save them, but you can help. Here are some resources you can turn to:

The *National Institute of Mental Health (NIMH)* (nimh.nih.gov) provides a wealth of up-to-date, accurate information about mental illness and has a "Health Topic" boxed link to Bipolar Disorder on its homepage.

National Alliance on Mental Illness (NAMI) (nami.org) offers information, support, and advocacy for people living with mental illness and their loved ones. In addition to their website, NAMI runs an information helpline at (800) 950-NAMI.

Psychology Today (psychologicaltoday.com) maintains a "Find a Therapist" link (for psychiatrists and counselors). While information is provided by the professionals themselves (and thus promotional), it can be a good place to start if you are looking for mental health care.

Focus on the Family (focusonthefamily.com) serves individuals and families with mental health issues by providing free phone counseling at: 1-855-771-4357 Monday through Friday between 6:00 a.m. and 8:00 p.m.

National Suicide Prevention Hotline (suicidepreventionlifeline.org) extends a 24-hour help line at: 1-800-273-8255. Their website also has a link for the deaf or hearing impaired.

Veterans Crisis Line (veteranscrisisline.net) cares for a rapidly increasing number of "wounded warriors" battling a wide variety of mental health issues. Their 24-hour hotline number is: 1-800-273-8255.

If you are at risk of hurting yourself or another, go to your local hospital emergency room.

Postlude - Delivered

One thing is sure: that underneath this sun
There is no new thing; age and age pass by;
The eye and ear are never satisfied
And every day ends like it has begun.
Tossed back and forth by blowing wind, we run
And gambol in the passing joy, yet sigh,
Caught in between the question and reply,
Tomorrow nothing new, today near done.
All this the Preacher saw and tells us now;
His findings – unresolved, vague – churn within.
Yet there is nothing better, he declares,
Than finding grateful joy in each affair,
Each orbit of this earth, each time therein,
And stand before our God, words few, and bow. [27]

~ "Joy in Each Season" by Matthew Pullar (After Christina
Rossetti's "The One Certainty")

The night this writing project was conceived, one of the
angels who seem to follow me around a good bit dropped
off a birthday card with a note inside which read, in part,

"As you may know, your birth date falls on the Memorial of
St. Anthony of Padua, a priest and doctor of the Roman
Catholic Church. In light of this, I'm sending you...the
readings which are used in the Liturgy of the Word in the
Mass held for that day."

Psalm 103 was one of these readings. In it, the Psalmist
engages in a little interior monologue quite familiar to those
of us who have battled various forms of mental illness. The

Psalmist then brings to mind the nature of the God we worship and adore. Our God is unchanging yet our experience of God is not. During periods of my life when I've been prone to self-loathing, I find comfort in the fact that –

He will not always accuse,
nor will he harbor his anger forever;
he does not treat us as our sins deserve
or repay us according to our iniquities.
For as high as the heavens are above the earth,
so great is his love for those who fear him;
as far as the east is from the west,
so far has he removed our transgressions from us. (Psalm 103:9-12)

The promise of God's marvelous mercy is enough to help me pass through the dark valleys that surround me, moving toward greener pastures ahead. It is enough to provide me shelter from the bright artificial glare that blinds me and keep me secure until I find peace and rest in God (not only in death, but in the land in the living). It is enough to keep me delighting in the Lord through the disorder of my mind.

Praise be to God in Jesus Christ!

Works Cited

(1) Robert Herrick, *Delight in Disorder* Works of Robert Herrick. vol I. Alfred Pollard, ed. London, Lawrence & Bullen, 1891. 32.

(2) Edward Arlington, *Richard Cory* (http://www.poetryfoundation.org/poem/174248)

(3) Sandi Patty, "You Are a Masterpiece" *Sandi Patti and the Friendship Company*, Word Music, 1989.

(4) Matthew Pullar, "He that made the ear" (http://mpullar.com/2013/04/25/he-that-made-the-ear-after-george-herberts-longing/)

(5) Matthew Pullar, "Buried Above the Ground" (http://mpullar.com/2013/05/13/buried-above-ground-after-william-cowpers-sapphics/)

(6) Timothy Keller, *The Prodigal God: Recovering the Heart of the Christian Faith*, Penguin 2008.

(7) Matthew Pullar, "The Bright-Shining Lord" (http://mpullar.com/2013/06/03/the-bright-shining-lord-after-ann-griffiths-i-saw-him-standing/)

(8) Jack London, *The Road and Other Stories* (http://www.online-literature.com/london/the-road/)

(9) Matthew Pullar, "Despair" (http://mpullar.com/2013/04/14/12-poets-1-despair-after-george-herberts-deniall/)

(10) Audio versions of various Bible translations are available at: biblegateway.com.

(11) Matthew Pullar, "Power Perfected in Weakness" (http://mpullar.com/2013/05/04/power-perfected-in-weakness-after-william-cowpers-light-shining-out-of-darkness/)

(12) Matthew Pullar, "Thanksgiving" (http://mpullar.com/2013/07/19/thanksgiving/)

(13) Matthew Pullar, "The Road" (http://mpullar.com/2013/07/04/the-road-after-christina-rossettis-uphill/)

(14) Kay Redfield Jamison, *An Unquiet Mind: A Memoir of Moods and Madness*, (Vintage Books 1995), 67.

(15) Ibid., 218

(16) Kathleeen Norris, *Acedia and Me: A Marriage, Monks, and a Writer's Life*, (Riverhead 2008), "Author's Note."

(17) Ibid., 3

(18) Katheryn Greene-McCreight, *Darkness Is My Only Companion: A Christian Response to Mental Illness*, (Brazos Press 2006), 21.

(19) Ibid., 31

(20) Ibid., 48

(21) Ibid., 49

(22) Sylvia Plath, *The Unabridged Journals of Sylvia Plath,* ed. Karen Kukil, (Anchor Books 2000), 43.

(23) Ibid., 29

(24) Ibid., 29

(25) Ibid., 31

(26) Ibid., 98

(27) Ibid., 59

(28) Ibid., 25

(29) Matthew Pullar, "Joy in Each Season" (http://mpullar.com/2013/07/12/joy-in-each-season-after-christina-rossettis-the-one-certainty/)

CPSIA information can be obtained
at www.ICGtesting.com
Printed in the USA
FFOW03n0916170314
4269FF